ZODIAC

North London

Edited by Simon Harwin

First published in Great Britain in 2002 by
YOUNG WRITERS
Remus House,
Coltsfoot Drive,
Peterborough, PE2 9JX
Telephone (01733) 890066

HB ISBN 0 75433 692 1
SB ISBN 0 75433 693 X

FOREWORD

Young Writers was established in 1991 with the aim of promoting creative writing in children, to make reading and writing poetry fun.

Once again, this year proved to be a tremendous success with over 41,000 entries received nationwide.

The Zodiac competition has shown us the high standard of work and effort that children are capable of today. The competition has given us a vivid insight into the thoughts and experiences of today's younger generation. It is a reflection of the enthusiasm and creativity that teachers have injected into their pupils, and it shines clearly within this anthology.

The task of selecting poems was a difficult one, but nevertheless, an enjoyable experience. We hope you are as pleased with the final selection in *Zodiac North London* as we are.

Contents

The Poems

A Homework Task - Writing A Poem

It's difficult for me to choose
A subject in which I can lose myself, express myself,
So I can address it,
Press it,
Impress,
So that you can hear and appreciate,
Opinionate,
Contemplate.

If I could I would
Express my thoughts, feelings, desires in a few brief words,
In a list of beautifully sculptured, perfectly rhyming words.

I'm not ignorant of my own ignorance,
How can I describe things
I don't understand?
My knowledge leaves me with the ability to describe an object,
Pretty perhaps,
Meaningful never.

I did try to address serious subjects,
World hunger,
Murder,
Terror,
Too typical, hypocritical.

I will try,
I'll think it over,
I will be braver,
I'll leave you on the edge of your seats,
Listening,
Silent with aspiration,
I need some bloody inspiration.

Joanna Clayton (14)
Acland Burghley School

Hen Hell

The stench of death
Is in the air,
For all we know
Our life is fair.
We live our lives
Shoved in a box,
There's no fear there
Of death by fox.

Nothing changes
Day by day,
We sit there cramped,
Just left to lay.
As weeks go on
The days grow cold,
The farmer says
We're getting old.

And so he packs
Us on a van;
He takes us to
A strange new land.
Then people hang us
Upside down
And their violence
Does astound.

The stench of death
Is in the air,
For all we know
All life is fair.
But it is not.
Death is not forced -
So end the chicken
Holocaust.

Jacob Bard-Rosenberg (15)
Acland Burghley School

CORRUPT

Mercilessly undone,
From their people they do abscond,
A not so forbidden fruit - more the carrot falsified,
Lacking lustre selfish - Idi Amin embracing cyanide,
Western immunity favoured over immune systems,
A bestowed fear, a prize worthy of callous values,
And what way forward?
Tribal Marxism falling short enough to scar first.

Countries far enough away to be free from lives,
Empathy unnecessary for trade beyond knives,
A continent ripe with prolonged tribes,
Exploited leaders rectified by arrogant scribes,
Ceaseless Western sustenance enough to sustain
And desert butchers too weak to refrain.

Tom Tabori (17)
Acland Burghley School

Frog Rock

I am a damp warm creature
with skin that's flat and elastic
I don't know about you, but frankly
my life is just fantastic
I like to climb up things
and I like my tree
but I don't much care for Tony Blair
or neo-Nazis or girl bands or Rolf Harris or
MTV.
No, I'm just perfectly happy
jumping up and down
saying 'ribbit'
and running round and round.
However
I'm not big on deforestation
or chemical warfare
or pollution
or concrete
or roads
or nuclear power
or landfills
or gamma rays
and you humans don't exactly have it great
either, what with . . .
fascism and
racism and
advertising and
AIDS and
ICBMs and
Echelon computers and
the IMF and
Geri and
Rolf and
ITV2 and
therefore

in conclusion
to this mental intrusion
I have to say
in every way
frogs beat humans any day
I've had it with Prog Rock
I prefer Frog Rock!

Owen Cryan (14)
Acland Burghley School

The Millipede

It's a polished worm
With a jointed armour
Each foot a tiny brush
Bunched up and swept forward
Like waves on the ocean
Lingering like drops of rain on your skin
Falling in a rhythmic pattern

As it clambers up my arm
Each nerve end tingles
The waves of legs propelling the millipede closer
The tide turns
The rain falls pointed needle-like and stabbing
Creeping up my arm
Nearing my elbow
Nerves dancing, heart racing
The waves become a tempest
Just get it off me!

Daniel Harrison (14)
Acland Burghley School

DAISY JAWS

Blood falls on the battlefield
the first hit has struck
now it can be seen who will yield
who will be in luck

I do not like this game
of gashes, wounds, and blood
for I am the first peaceful
and tame
to ever grace the mud

I am not one for war
not one for vicious fights
I prefer relaxing on the floor
and watching stars at night

They laugh at me and call me names
like dung and daisy jaws
they say I'm crazy and insane
but I don't care about my flaws

So hopefully one day
once the fighting has stopped
they will see my way
when the last blood has dropped.

Sacha Coward (14)
Acland Burghley School

POEM SONG

The binds are home,
The air is long,
That's why I wrote this lovely song.
The air is fresh,

The moon is light,
That's the star that will light up the night.
The morning is as light
As a yellow spring sunflower.

Jesse Pitfield (11)
Acland Burghley School

The Tree Frog

Clinging to the tree
arms stretching
tightly
a crushed embrace

Eyes twinkle
dull yellow orbs
a single black melon seed
set in a ring of gold

Cold and clammy
the throat throbs
its creamy under belly
bulges
on each intake of breath

Leaping
legs stretch like elastic
exposing small feet
gummy toes like suction cups
colours
mixing and dancing
like an ocean.

Tom Gillie (13)
Acland Burghley School

UNTITLED

She sleeps as I cry
Oblivious and deaf to the
Sound of my pain
But she must never know
She must never see
She must never hear my thoughts
For she is happy now
I sit alone in the world
All around me is colour but the
Pain takes mine away
And all that is left is
A plain black and white life
The fire and passion she possesses
Will never penetrate the layers of life between us
But my tears begin to melt the eternal void
And from time to time she looks up and smiles
And I know she is getting closer.

Alice Fodor (17)
Acland Burghley School

PETRARCHAN SONNET

They say it's not over till the fat lady sings. Last night
She sung. A line is now drawn between your heart and mine,
And the link that we once made is now hard to define.
Our paths will still cross but no longer will they weave so tight,
And although I shall miss you I shall try with all of my might
Never to cry or to tell everybody I'm fine.
I will smile when I see you and never give out any sign

That inside me there's something still burning too hard to fight,
And I hate myself 'cause you couldn't love who I was,
But I'll never forget the time I spent wrapped in your arms.
I hope that one day someone will see that they want me again
And they'll pick up the pieces of me that you left, because
Without you I'll stay somewhere safe where I can't be harmed,
Where no one can cause me anymore hurt or pain.

Georgie Donati (16)
Acland Burghley School

THE LEOPARD

He chases you and never gives up,
Never lets you go,
His sharp claws are like forks,
He runs like a train,
He eats deer,
He is brightly coloured,
He has black spots and orange skin,
He sprints faster than ever,
Chases his prey fiercely until,
Finally he stops.
Rests for a while,
Then catches his eye on another deer,
He goes running over and . . .
The deer is dead,
The leopard sucks the blood with his red tongue
And slowly eats it up.

Sean Ritchie (11)
Acland Burghley School

TANGLED IN MISERY

Like a pawn trapped in my own nightmare
All in a bath of blue, cold air
Filthy fingernails ripping at my stare
In my wild game of truth or dare

With my head full of hopes and
My mouth full of strawberries
As I swallow the sun
With my face up in the clouds
Perfection came undone . . .
My heart just breathes ashes
Yet there's fire in my mind . . .
Because nothing's forgotten
In this world of backward time

This world which *hates*
And rarely smiles
Each flower spits blood on Heaven's
Sundial
This winter shine storm
A world of glass, a globe of clear grey
Remember nothing yet fear your dying day

Once in a while we can crawl out
Of the slop, hose ourselves off
And pretend to be human beings again
. . . But my star is fading
And I don't know what to do
From gold to blue
From gold to murky, dirty blue.

Jess Mayne (16)
Acland Burghley School

Snake

A perfect sunset over the sea
His skin shines like stained silk
Eyes like hot embers
A scaled body, long and thin
He is polished wood, cool and smooth
But the colours of a cornfield of caramel
A void of cool fire
And a tongue like a flickering flame
Slithering slowly, softly, silently
Searching for food
That's when he stops . . .
Catching the scent of a field mouse
He sweeps across the ground
Speedily sneaking towards his unwary prey
He's been seen
His shiny skin caught the light
That's when he strikes
It falls to the floor
Two wounds to its neck
His teeth turn back like jagged daggers
His twelve day fast ended.

Sam Wilson (14)
Acland Burghley School

School

In school you must make sure you listen,
Or you'll turn out like Johnny Briston,
You'll sing and fart,
And act like a tart,
With your brain as soft as a cushion.

Thomas Jones (11)
Acland Burghley School

KETCHUP THE CORN SNAKE

Butter-yellow and scarlet honeycomb skin
Feels like a roll of oily dough in cling film.
Graceful in movement but sleepy, detached
I've been here before, it thinks
Inquisitive tongue darts out, then vanishes
Head, tail coils moves
Red and yellow stripes slide
Over, under and past each other
It flows to the floor
Over the mat
Eyes searching
Two crimson beads
Fuzzily scan the room
The tongue flicks out once more
Tasting grey library carpet
The handler retrieves it
And the snake vanishes into the blue cloth bag
Gone.

Owen Kennedy (15)
Acland Burghley School

LEE

There once was a young boy called Lee
Who wasn't too fat or skinny.
He was right in the middle,
As straight as a fiddle
And as silly as silly could be.

Lee Perkins (11)
Acland Burghley School

KETCHUP

The moment of truth
It's in my hands
Curling round and round
The skin is greasy
The eyes are red
Moving without a sound
The colour's dusty
The honeycombed skin
The gentle embrace of a snake
The movements deliberate
The knowing look
It's gone now, away, it's here no more
Leaving memories in its wake.

Adam Price (14)
Acland Burghley School

A SNAKE

Orchestra
of millions of
tiny, hard scales
together they are so smooth
soft, silky
she is calm, aloof
but ready to act
alert
she is beautiful
powerful
I am cautious
I am honoured
I am in awe.

Rose Leadbeater (14)
Acland Burghley School

TRYING TO WRITE A SONNET

Weary am I, to what lies straight ahead,
Does yonder sunlight shine upon my path,
Will darkness blind sweet precious sun? I dread
Will my vision alter, me mumble, laugh?
To panic? In circumstances like these
Normal, when mind spins spirals within squares
Scratches, fading sounds! Do they come from trees
From the forest? Who will enter, who dares?
Releasing one's fear escapes a trapped soul,
Then truth can be centre of attention.
Fear, repetitive sounds, where's the control?
A sharp-edged tool! Tree has new dimensions.
  Experiments bring interesting delights,
  Not all that lies ahead is purely white.

Janica Dennison (17)
Acland Burghley School

9 O'CLOCK

At nine o'clock the cry goes out
It's bedtime, without a doubt
It's nine o'clock, it's very late
But I still do really hate
At nine o'clock the cry goes out,
Please, not bedtime yet, he says with doubt.

Elliot Thomas (11)
Acland Burghley School

MUNDANE MONDAY

Tucked in for the night she sleeps.
Each breath follows a tremble and a shudder.
Clothed from head to toe I see her eyes
Half open, slits avoiding the outside world.

The cardboard boxes are her castle, raised high to surround her,
Protection from the night and occult weather.
She is the princess in her tower, except her dream is short,
Lasts only until she is thrown from a doorstep.
Another bedrock must be found to fabricate her life.

The strongest woman in the world.

Plastic bags to keep her dry
She must fight to protect her spot against the dark angel who has come to take her away.
Not ready, she is bound with rags,
And the cardboard boxes her castle, raised high to surround her.

I know when she will surrender,
When times become too easy
No challenge to boggle her mind
Just a mundane Monday.
The day she is looked upon in pity.

Tamara Hutchinson (18)
Ashmole School

DARK WEDDING

The crowd comes marching in:
Swift, swift, swift -

Black chiffon and butterfly-patterned lace -
Obscure and obsolete.
She marks a new wedding night.

Suited in black they come marching through
Two by two
Holding a long black leather box in mid-air.

A sheet of black lace lies softly
Upon the dead.

Buds of black roses scattered along the path:
Thorny and ferocious -
They lay the path for the newly wedded couple.

Leading into a new life
Of darkness.

Like a circus, but without smiles
Or laughter, or cheers -
All - except the bride - in her frail enigmatic smile.

Butterflies - dark and fragile
They scattered upon the bride
Suffocating her passion, her hopes, her life . . .

Then away they flew searching for their next target -
Hear their imminence:
Swift, swift, swift -

Charmaine Yiman Chan (18)
Ashmole School

I WISH I COULD FLY

Flying high in early May
I feel the freeness birds feel every day
Slipping from breeze to breeze
Soaring over the trees
I look up at the sky
I wish I could fly.

Katherine Bennett (17)
Ashmole School

JOURNEYS

A journey can be far and wide,
To see it close, look deep inside.
It can be short, it can be long,
It can be a bridge standing strong.
Like China and Japan, that's really far,
Also like a shooting star.
It can be high, it can be low,
It can be fast, it can be slow.
A journey can be big, a journey can be small,
A journey can be short, a journey can be tall.
I make a journey to my house, I know it off by heart,
It's just a little road that never splits apart.
A journey is Heaven, a very long path,
It can make you sad, it can make you laugh.
A journey can be a flash that you never see,
Turning into a girl and a lady.
Just remember a journey is just a part of life,
Like from a baby to a wife.

Maleaka Brathwaite-Quire (11)
Convent of Jesus and Mary RC School

The Seven Ages Of A Woman

(A response to the Seven Ages of a Man by William Shakespeare)

Our life is like an unexplained story
All the people we love or hate
Belong to this story.
Just like a story it has different chapters
A story with seven chapters.

It starts
A little baby crawling in a pink dress
Trying to pull off the matching ribbons on her head
Next, her mother is waving goodbye as the little girl
Enters the school for the first time.

Now she is a young girl with mixed emotions,
Her body is changing
And she is falling in love
But with who, she can't decide.

She has just finished her University degree
Settling down in her new job.
The fifth chapter starts,
She is now married and has three lovely children,
She still goes to work
But she is more committed to her family.

She is nearly at the end of her book
She has retired happily,
All her children have finished school and have their own families.

In her last chapter,
She lies on her bed dreaming of the last
Six chapters of her life,
The good times and the bad,
This time when she wakes up she will be with God in Heaven,
As her book is complete.

Marian Tawafig (14)
Convent of Jesus and Mary RC School

COMING BACK FROM FLORIDA

Coming back from Florida
to the dark and dreary rain,
I went to tell my mother,
she said 'Oh what a pain.'

Coming back from lovely white sand
and waves which hit the rocks,
then I looked at the weather forecast
and it gave me quite a shock.

It took us twelve hours to get there
even with three hours' delay
and when we finally got on board,
we shouted 'Hip hip hooray!'

The stewards and the air crew
were really very nice,
they reassured me on my first flight
that I was going to be fine.

When we finally got to our hotel,
I gave a great big grin,
because on the massive outside sign
it said 'The Holiday Inn'.

On my fantastic holiday we had:
Fun in the sun, when the good times begun,
we had adventures in places like
Seaworld and Universal Studios.
I could keep going and never stop, never,
but all I can say is
this was the best holiday ever.

Sophie Elisabeth Dean (11)
Convent of Jesus and Mary RC School

My Poem About School

As I sit in class,
Staring at the board,
Listening to the laughter and the roars.
These wooden tables,
Those rock-hard chairs,
I know they're not comfortable,
But who cares.
Students in uniform is what I can see,
Walking along the corridor staring at me,
Sitting at the front in a sophisticated suit,
Is the head of the class,
Wearing shiny new boots.
Period one, period two, period three, four, five,
So much to do, I want to curl up and hide,
Then when it's all over, I can go back to form,
So that Miss can do the register and we can all go home.

Claire Louise Kellegher (13)
Convent of Jesus and Mary RC School

Journey

Going on a journey is really, really fun,
You can make one through to Africa
And also one to Hong Kong.

It could either be to work,
Or drop your kids at school,
But wherever you'll be going, you'll be
Making one or two.

It could be sunny in one place,
But rainy in another,
You can always drive to your gran's house,
And go undercover.

So there you are,
Journeys, journeys, journeys!
Some people love them but some people don't,
Which one shall you pick, car or boat?

Sesen Ghezai (11)
Convent of Jesus and Mary RC School

MY TRAIN JOURNEY

Step onto the train,
I'm tired and grumpy, I just want to sit down,
See a seat with my name.
The people are looking at me with a frown,
I get out my book,
I try to relax,
I give them a look,
I go back to my book.

The train's rushing past,
I feel great,
The green of the grass,
I just can't wait,
I open the window, the wind hits my face,
Good clean fresh air and I take it with grace.

Sarah-Nell Moullier (11)
Convent of Jesus and Mary RC School

My Journey To Space

I was in a spaceship
Flying by, way, way up in the sky
Then I turned my head
And suddenly saw
A moving star upon us all
It was glazing around
In the dark warm night
And gave everyone a stunning sight
It glazed about
With no fear at all
While all the others
Stood up and adored
Oh I wish I could be
That star up in space
I'd be the centre of attention
And everyone would praise.

Keisha Bascoe (11)
Convent of Jesus and Mary RC School

Where?

Where can a lonely person
Find a willing friend?
Where can a broken loving heart
Find its love again?

Where can we find our forgotten love
To the greatest person above?
Where can we express how we feel
When we are stuck at home eating our meal?

Where can people in the war
Find the way out through the peace door?
Where can those with a guilty heart
Gain their true love and never again depart?

Where can I find my destination
Through the closed doors of life's new creation?
Where can I find the true inspiration
When the doors are shut to all communication?

Sandra Tawafig (13)
Convent of Jesus and Mary RC School

JOURNEYS

Fly to Jamaica
for sun and the sea
smell the ice creams ready to be eaten

Fly to England
for wind and rain
see and hear the children play

Fly to the North Pole
for ice and snow
smell a rotten carrot of a snowman's nose

Fly to Spain
for parties on the beach
feel the sand burning your feet

You can fly anywhere in the world
the weather hot or cold.

Kelsie O'Connor (11)
Convent of Jesus and Mary RC School

CONVENT GIRL

When I look into the mirror,
Who do I see?
A little convent girl looking at me.
Dressed in blue from head to toe
And on her hair a little blue bow.
Laughing, playing, being cheerful,
Never crying, never tearful.
Starting secondary school was a bit of a scare,
First she thought it was just not fair.
Meeting new teachers,
All with different features.
At the end of the day she had a friend called Faye,
They got on well,
They met after the lunch bell.
First they had technology
And after that, biology.
In art they made a card,
They worked very hard.
Then passed September, October, November
And all up to next year.
Now she's in year eight
And Faye is still her mate.
Now when I look into the mirror,
Who do I see?
A big convent girl looking at me.

Zynab Al-Kadhim (12)
Convent of Jesus and Mary RC School

JOURNEYS

The train slides into the platform,
A morning bundle of people push their way through the crowds,
The platform covered in sheets of people,
Busy office men and women chatting on their mobiles.

Huddling along, pushing, shoving,
Going in different directions,
All on a journey, where will it end?
London, Edinburgh, Paris, Rome,
All around the world,
All on a journey.

Fiona Bond (11)
Convent of Jesus and Mary RC School

A JOURNEY? YES, A JOURNEY

Whilst saying a rhyme, I'll step back in time
And take a journey.
A journey? Yes, a journey.
Where is it to? Is it through the air?
No, it's a trip to London. Yeah!
To London, yes, to London
Or maybe even the London Dungeons.
Want to go to the Millennium Wheel or
Even go to the farm and hear the pigs squeal.
The sheep are asleep,
I'd like one to keep!
The chickens and hens
Are locked in their pens.
The dog's on the hill
With a farmer called Bill.
The farmer's wife, Mayble,
Locked the horses in the stable.
It's getting late
And I'm meeting my mum at the gate
And take a long journey home.
A journey? Yes, a journey.

Jannine Uppal (11)
Convent of Jesus and Mary RC School

In Loving Memory Of My Nan!

(RIP Nan, who died 1/3/00)

Nan I love you
and I know you love me
I wish we could be a happy family
now that you're gone
I wish we were one.

I know you're in Heaven
looking down on me
but it's not the way we used to be.
You'll always be in my heart and mind
I'll always remember how you were so kind
I'll never forget the song we sang
and when I'd talk to you when the phone rang
I wish I could've said 'Bye'
But I also wish I could say 'Hi.'

Rachel Ford (13)
Convent of Jesus and Mary RC School

Out Of My House

Out of my house, into the cold and wet.
Out of my house, ready for a long walk.
Into school, out of the cold and wet.
Into school, ready for a long day.

Out of my house to breathe in the fresh air.
Out of my house, starting a clean day at school.
Out of my house, ready to see my friends.
Into school to see my teachers.
Into school, ready for my homework.
Into school to start my work.

Michelle Louise Rosario (11)
Convent of Jesus and Mary RC School

A Journey To Italy

My plane left at 6am
The sight was cold and daring
With black clouds surrounding the plane
As I felt a cold breeze on my back
I flew up through the clouds
Passing the dark, wet clouds from which we flew up
It was fluorescent, bright, as it was sunny at last
Which had caught my eye
Flying over and over, twisting and turning
All of a sudden my stomach started doing the same
But relief, I was nearly going to leave the plane
As we were landing, I was so happy to see Italy
At last at 12am.

Jessica Kovacs (12)
Convent of Jesus and Mary RC School

My Journey

(Inspired by Grace Nichols' Out of Africa)

Out of England, cold and windy.
Out of England, trains and buses.
Out of England, chips and burger.
Out of England, sad and happy.
Out of England, friends and neighbours.

Into Jamaica, sun and rain.
Into Jamaica, taxis and minibuses.
Into Jamaica, ackee and saltfish.
Into Jamaica, fun and exciting,
Into Jamaica, family and friends.

Samantha Mary Senior (11)
Convent of Jesus and Mary RC School

IRELAND

We pack our bags to go to Ireland,
We read our magazines in the car to go to Ireland,
We travel on the boat to go to Ireland,
We all just love Ireland.

We're here in Ireland now,
We look out the window in Ireland,
We see green fields with cows munching on the grass in Ireland,
We all just love Ireland.

The weather is never sunny but wet in Ireland,
We go galloping on our horses across the green fields in Ireland,
We sit in front of the orange and yellow fire,
Keeping our hands and feet warm,
We all just love Ireland.

Kayleigh Kilcommons (11)
Convent of Jesus and Mary RC School

JOURNEYS

I'm going on a journey, I'm going far away,
I'm going on a journey, I'm going there today.
I'm going somewhere hot
And I hope to see a lot.
I'm bringing a mate
And it's going to be great.
I'm going to sunny Spain, but it's a pain,
I've got too much luggage and I'm going insane.
I've got there at last,
The journey went fast.
Wow! Spain is breathtaking.

Ellen Morrissey (11)
Convent of Jesus and Mary RC School

WIND

Breeze is a transparent friend
Small and white
Harms no one or creature
Just touches and becomes your friend
Her hands touch your face
She makes you feel calm
But when she becomes upset
She transforms to Wind!

Wind is a see-through bully
Nothing like Breeze
He punches and kicks
Harder than a squeeze
He loves to pick
To choose his creature
But he selects far too well
Changes the world's features
To him, like picking up a bell.

He batters houses
He tortures flats
He boxes trees
And he thumps leaves

So when you see Breeze
Just be very pleased
Don't be upset
You don't know what else
Could be behind breeze.

Connie Ip (12)
Copthall School

The Emotional Sky

Sky is a moody, emotional person,
always changing his mind.

One minute Sky is peaceful and snowing,
little frosty, silver sparks swishing
down like a light, shiny, silver feather.

Suddenly huge Hail reigns down,
marching in his private army.
Thumping windows, knocking on doors.

Soon thumping fades, you only hear
Rain dripping down.
Singing her song 'pitter-patter, pitter-patter'
she sings herself to sleep.

In the dull, dark night, Sky turns on
his bright, powerful lamp; glowing Sun
shares light with Earth.

Sky gives his rare colourful smile;
a shimmering beautiful rainbow.

Razia Jaffer (12)
Copthall School

My Pencil Case, Mrs Cosmic Babe

Mrs Cosmic Babe
Was opened out of her packet,
All her body parts were in it,
So she could not fidget.

Mrs Cosmic Babe's pretty face smiled,
Mrs Cosmic Babe's face looked mild.
Mrs Cosmic Babe's long hair on her head
Made Mrs Cosmic Babe look red.

Mrs Cosmic Babe gets knocked off a happy cliff,
She gets knocked over by someone stiff.
A lady giant from far, far away
Comes back and saves the day.

Mrs Cosmic Babe is knocked around,
Till the day she is found.
See her in the sea,
She is buzzing like a bee.

Yvonne Mutale (12)
Copthall School

Whitey The Clock

Whitey the clock never stops,
Drinks tea or rubs his knee,
Tick-tock day and night,
His arrow pointing,
His bright face, white.

Tells the time,
Never whines,
Can't move
Or pound on the ground,
Looking at Moon, also round.

All alone he moans and groans,
Listening to the day and night sounds,
Always awake, nearly silent,
Listening for creaks and leaks.

Only friend is Mouse,
Who climbs about,
At 3am running from the cat,
Inside Whitey, Mouse sat.

Katy Ho (12)
Copthall School

The Sun

Sun you are a coin dropping down Heaven's drain
You are revolving the Earth like a golden train
Sun you sometimes glisten in my eye
Shining high up in the sky

Sun you give us a smile and a grin
You put up your chin
You smile and glow in space
Bringing a smile to every face

Sun you are a fiery ball
Spinning round and round
Your black patterns on the ground
Make not a squeak or a sound

You're a yellow sphere
Awake in the morning
And asleep in the night
A day without you
Would be a day without light.

Farhana Uddin (12)
Copthall School

Weatherman

Clouds grow grey with anger,
As they beam bright flashing lights.
Wind strokes gently, whistling at the window
And Sky spits sharp daggers in the black of night.

Rain pats gently on the roof,
As the whiteness of snow walks the land,
Trailing her white cape behind her,
Leaving a chill from the touch of her hand.

Sun's orange glow overpowers the anger of grey
And brightness streaks across the sky,
Anger and cold elapse to their last seconds,
Only to shrivel up and die.

Laura Horwich (12)
Copthall School

THE SUN

Sun is like a mother
Watching over us,
Keeping us warm
In the winter months.
Tanning our face and
Burning our skin,
Better to be outside
Than staying in.

Making us happy
When days are dull,
Making us bright
When times are dim.
Giving us light,
Making us bright,
Perfect for a barbecue
On a Saturday night.

But at the end of the day
When Sun goes in,
We sigh and think that soon
Mother will be back again.

Lauren Thomas (12)
Copthall School

MY SIMILE POEM

Just look at this, it's me,
I'm as shiny as the stars
And as bright as day.
I can sing like a lark
And bite like a shark.
I'm as free as a bird
And can always be heard!

I can be cold as ice,
But also be warm and nice.
I can be really colourful,
Just like a rainbow,
But also be murky grey,
When people shout and say
Rude names.

So I'm shiny and bright,
Can be cold and can be nice,
Be really colourful and grey
And can be heard through the day.

So listen everybody, this is me,
I believe it and you will,
Can't you see?

Dolly Latilo (11)
Copthall School

THE SNOW QUEEN

The Snow Queen is a cold person,
White-haired, white-skinned and blue-lipped,
She sends down frozen cotton wool,
Appearing from her sharpened fingertips.

As Snow falls through the sky,
Cackling on the green grass she'll lie.
Soon she is eaten away,
But the frosty Snow Queen will return another day.

Nadia Mayhew (12)
Copthall School

COLOURS!

Black as your heart when you see only bad,
Emotions are upside-down.
Black is the world when your heart is not free,
The ice must be broken and feelings be found.

Red as the anger that builds up inside,
Or the love that fills your heart.
Feelings, emotions are tossing and turning,
Hatred and love are combined.

White as your mind, so blank and bleak,
The words are spinning around.
Distressed, but happy, muddled inside,
Your body and mind are weak.

Blue as your soul, the way you feel,
When nothing is going right.
But if you turn against those feelings inside,
Happiness will be a great sight.

Pink is the colour of glee and of joy,
The moment that nothing is lost.
Be happy, rejoice and let out a squeal,
For happiness, there is no cost.

Jessie Wand (12)
Copthall School

Guess Who?

Wind blower
Tantrum thrower

Sand storm
My form

Hear me whisper
Hear me scream

Grass cutter
Mad nutter

Sunlight beam
Drama queen

Hear me whisper
Hear me scream

Wildlife lover
Respects my mother

Bush shaper
Crying faker

Hear me whisper
Hear me scream

Moonlight
Great in a fight

Mountain peak
Asleep for a week

Hear me whisper
Hear me scream

Guess who?

Me?

Zoe Margaret Harris (11)
Copthall School

INDEPENDENT WOMEN!

Nobody knows how much I love my family,
I carry them in my mind,
I tell them everything in life
And I help them a lot too,
Of course I'll never forget them!

Nobody knows friends like mine,
Especially when we give each other presents
And huddle around together,
Share our gruesome stories
And stay good friends forever!

Nobody can eat my food,
Especially the way I stuff it in my mouth,
A bowl of chips and a dip of ketchup
Is a delicious meal I like,
Of course I will have a burger on the side!

When there are no shadows around me,
I am standing there lonely,
Trying to keep calm, because . . .
There's only one of me!

Purvi Doshi (11)
Copthall School

There Isn't . . .

There isn't another one of me,
There is only me.
There isn't a head with the same kind of brain,
There is only my brain.
There isn't a person with the look of love when they see their family,
There is only my look of love.
There isn't a person with the taste of sweetness
When they bite into an apple,
There is only my taste of sweetness.
There isn't a person who laughs my laugh and talks the talk that I do,
There is only my laugh and talk.

There isn't a person in this universe
Who looks and is like me.

If you don't understand then read each little verse
And then you would really see.

Even if they have a similar name,
We are not a weenie bit the same.

Angy Elsaghir (11)
Copthall School

Me

Just look at this, it's me!
I'm as sweet as a child,
Yet graceful as a swan,
I'm as bright as a daffodil,
Blooming in the sun.

I'm as light as a blossom,
Floating to the ground,
I'm as quiet as a mouse,
Never to make a sound,
That's me!

Heena Rehman (11)
Copthall School

About Me

Nobody else has my looks,
I have black hair,
I have hazel brown eyes,
I am short.

Nobody else has my feelings,
My eyes go watery,
My voice gets dry,
My face is unhappy.

Nobody else knows my emotions,
I get really upset,
I go to my room and start sobbing,
I can't cry if someone is standing.

I can't stand my emotions,
Nobody else laughs like me,
I keep myself happy,
I make my cousins laugh
And try to cheer up my family.

Taibah Shabir (12)
Copthall School

My Simile Poem About Me!

Just look at this,
It's me!
As elegant as a swan
With long golden silky hair,
Chatty like a parrot,
As lively as a lion,
Calm like the sea,
As cute as a rabbit,
Fast like the wind,
You never see me,
Small like a pea,
Even though I'm very loud,
With a fragrance like a rose,
But I never like to pose,
Sweeter than a sweet,
With little tiny feet,
Strong like an ox,
As busy as an ant,
Fit as a fiddle,
Just look over here,
It's me, it's me.

Holly Webster (11)
Copthall School

It's Me!

Just look at me
This is me
My skin is as soft as a peach
My eyes are as blue as the beach
My hair shines like gold in the sunlight
Sometimes I feel as wild as a lion

But I would like to be as friendly as a teacher
I like jumping like a kangaroo
I like swimming like a dolphin
As neat as my best handwriting
And everyone can see
That I am a funny person, me!

Sarah Cooper (11)
Copthall School

MYSELF

My eyes are greeny-brown, my hair is light brown,
Shoulder length with a fringe that makes me want to frown.

My height is 5ft, average for a girl my age,
My weight is normal at this stage.

My skin is pale, I would love a tan,
That cannot be helped, I am what I am.

I look like my mother, oh what a pity,
Only joking, she's quite pretty.

I have a naughty brother, who is going to be three years old,
When I was his age, I was as good as gold.

My household consists of three,
Mother, brother and me.

My nan and papa live a few doors down,
What a pleasure to have them around.

My grandfather lives a few miles away,
Oh! If he could only stay.

Stephanie Pearce (11)
Copthall School

THERE IS ONLY ONE ME

Nobody can have the pleasure like me when I put my gold studs in,
Nobody can have the pleasure like me when I put my trousers on,
There is only one me.

Nobody knows my family the way I do,
Nobody knows how annoying my sister is,
There is only one me.

Nobody knows the pleasure I feel when I eat a bowl of chips,
Nobody knows how much I love chocolate, I love it a lot,
There is only one me.

Nobody's felt the way I felt when I walked the streets of New York,
Nobody's had the same joy as me when on the horse in
Dean's open farm,
There is only one me.

Nobody can ever be like me,
I am one individual person.

Charlotte Mary Day (11)
Copthall School

SIMILE ABOUT ME

Just look at this, it's me, it's me,
I'm as graceful as a swan,
But I can be as sly as a fox,
It's me the chatterbox girl,
I'm as soft as a rabbit's fur,
But I can be as hard as a rock,

It's Aisha, the big, tall pisha,
I'm as fast as a cheetah,
But as tall as a giraffe,
It's her again, the sportiest girl you've seen,
It's me and now you know my true self.

Aisha Kamara (11)
Copthall School

Me In The World!

You can't love your family the way I do,
There is only my love.
You can't copy who I am,
There is only my copy.

You can't look the way I look,
There is only my look.
You can't run as fast as I can,
There is only my type of running.

You can't talk the way I talk,
There is only my voice.
You can't think my thoughts,
There are only my thoughts.

You can't laugh the way I laugh,
There is only my laugh,
You can't be me because there is only one of
Me!

Kuziva Foroma (11)
Copthall School

WHO I AM?

Who I was,
I was a different person to that I am today.
That was a perfect life,
But the perfect life has been torn away from me.
I have grown, I now know that no one understands my feelings.
I now know that no one has the time to talk to me
And know who I am.

There is only one person who came up to me and gave me a chance
And from the experience I will never feel the same as that person again,
She is a true friend, I will remember her today and forever.

I have never been good at sport but as my teacher says,
'Try your best.'
But that wasn't the only problem, it was when it came to picking sides,
I was the last of them all,
It was like everyone always picks vegetables last to eat,
It ended up like I was the vegetable, last to be picked.

There is only one of me,
Nobody has the same fingerprint,
Nobody thinks the way I do,
Nobody has my life,
I have something that if you lost it, it couldn't be replaced,
That something I have is my life,
Others might find theirs special but I don't.

Purvi Shah (11)
Copthall School

Mr Rain

He brews up in the clouds
Creeping and crunching out
He's ready to be loud
Tit tat
Tat tit
All he does is spit and spit

He's hiding behind some candyfloss clouds
Drumming at the shiny sun
He's taunting, panting, yelling out.
'I'm the number one!'
He calms down, quiet and soft.
His wetness shivers away,
But he's resting and waiting
For another day.
Zzzzz.

Abra Dark (12)
Copthall School

The Rain

Sky cried raindrops
Splish, splash slowly down
Rain pours down
Rain, you frown
Rain you cry, cry
Drumming at the windows
Pitter-patter, pitter-patter
A 'drummin' dreadful noise to listen to
Rain why are you upset?

Parita Shah (12)
Copthall School

THE BLAZING SUN

Sun is a blazing, angry woman
Always in a temper.
Burning brightly in the sky,
Higher than the clouds,
She waits until Day has gone,
Before she slows her flames down.

Then she waits a little while
To light her flames again,
She beats Rain,
Finds him a pain,
Rain's cold and gloomy
And she's bright and blooming.
She does this all over again,
Until forever ends.

Adelena Caranese (12)
Copthall School

THE SUN

The sun is like a ball of fire
Gleaming in the daylight
The sun is a happy face that sits high in the sky
Peering at everyone as they go by.

It's a friend of the rain
An enemy of thunder
It has rays of happiness and light
Touching everyone's lives
Without you we would not be
Alive!

Daniella Wright (12)
Copthall School

THE ORANGE TREE

Hanging from a green thread,
Sometimes you could believe they're dead,
Green, to yellow, to orange,
Happier by the minute.

Slowly they form a vast smile,
Widen their sides with juice,
Seed to fruit,
Awake with the morning glow.

Their orange cheeks smile with glee,
Sweet, to sour, to ripe,
Drinking in the rain.

Until they drop to a green bed,
Rotting by the cold sky,
Orange, to green, to nothing at all,
Asleep, but not alone.

Naomi Beckett (12)
Copthall School

THE SNOWDROP FLOWER

Snow! You sprinkled sugar over my bare meadows,
You stretched out a sheet over my sleeping garden.

You stroked the bush with your icy fingers,
You kissed the holly with your frozen lips,
You are the Snow Queen dancing with Winter,
You flit daintily as a snowdrop flower.

Your coconut shavings shoulder each other,
Creating a glistening, gleaming, cover.

Sarah Douglas (12)
Copthall School

The Eating Sea

The sea has spiky claws
As well as sharp clashing jaws
He has lots of hairs
And two pairs
Of what?
Eyes, ears and wings
He swings
Happily
Forwards
Backwards
Has an enormous mouth
Lives all the way down south
His mouth which we call a beak
Always squeaks
This rocky special seat
Is where he always eats
Chewing at the cliffs
With a big grin on his face.

Maryam Ali (12)
Copthall School

Rain

Rain is a drummer pounding down on our homes,
Rain you're a big blue bully bashing on our faces,
Rain you're an angry child stamping his feet,
When you're tired you crawl away with your dismal face down.

The day is clear, sun shines and
Rain sleeps like a babbling baby.

Roxanna Boromand (12)
Copthall School

Just Look At Me!

As if a blowing tree
Just how I'd like to be
Delicate like a swan
Soft as a feather
Cold like the weather
Fast as a cheetah
Invisible like the air
As rich as the mayor
Colourful like a bird
I think my birthday is on the third
As furry as a dog
Skinny like a small log
Lumpy like a frog
As cheeky as a cat
Flat like a mat
I may seem boring
But trust me, I'm not.

Jade Perrin (11)
Copthall School

The Sun

Sun's sweaty brow turns
the morning sun silver with dew.
Sun's hot fists beat on the ground
and turn the mud into soil.
Sun's smile lights up the dead streets.
Sun's bright eyes sparkle in the sea.
Sun's warm arms wrap around the children.
Sun's glowing back sets on another day.

Marina Athanasi (12)
Copthall School

My Poem About Me

Look at me
Hair black as coal
Skin yellow as
A baked potato
Nose flat as
A chocolate pancake
Sometimes I'm loud
As an elephant
Other times quiet
As a mouse
Skinny as a stick
Eyes black as charcoal
Fit as a fiddle
Embarrassed
I'm as red as an apple
That's me!

Katie Ma (11)
Copthall School

The Sun

You are so fun to be with,
To be with you for a day would be great,
You help me feel better when I feel down.

You're so beautiful, big and orange,
You follow me through the day
And wake me up in the morning.

You're my best friend, you play with me,
We play follow the leader
And hide and seek you always win.

Heather Briancourt (12)
Copthall School

I Am

They say I'm . . .
As quiet as a pin
As solemn as a mouse
As sweet as candy
Long and dangly

As moody as my sister
As whingy as a baby
As sulky as a pregnant lady

Though I'm similar to many
I can honestly say
I'm a unique being
That won't ever change.

Hope Levine (11)
Copthall School

Me

Skin as bright as a peach,
Eyes like autumn leaves,
Lips as red as cherries,
Arms like branches of a tree,
Legs like hockey sticks,
Feet like rubber balls,
A temper like a raging fire,
But inside I'm like jelly,
Like an everlasting laughing teddy,
That's me!
That's me!
That's me!

Josephine Smith (11)
Copthall School

JUST LOOK AT ME!

Just look at this,
It's me,
I ebb and flow like the sea,
This is how I want to be.

Like a parrot, I'm cheeky,
Like a dolphin, I'm clever,
Like a cheetah, I'm fast
And like a hyena, I love to laugh!

I'm as loud as an elephant
And sometimes as quiet as a mouse,
I like to be known to be as sweet as a flower.

As a singing bird, I like to sing
And as elegant as a swan,
I like to swim.

Koren O'Leary (11)
Copthall School

IT'S ME!

Just look at this!
It's me! It's me!
As graceful as a swan,
As loud as a lion, you see?
As sly as a fox,
As slow as a snail,
As cheerful as a hyena,
Like a leopard on the run,
Sometimes a lyin' in the sun,
It's me! It's me!

Lindsey Brand (11)
Copthall School

Look At This

Look at this!
It's me
I'm as busy as a bee
And nearly as brown as a berry
My eyes are like the shells of hazelnuts
I can feel as tall as giraffe
Or as small as an ant
I'm like a teacher
Always patient
I swim like a fish
I'm springy like a rubber band
That is it
That's what I am.

Azadeh Bozorgmanesh-Fard (12)
Copthall School

It's Me

Just look at this,
It's me!
Sometimes bright as day
And sometimes dull as grey.
Energetic like a dancer,
Leaping gracefully,
Eyes are brown like a grizzly bear
And I always care.
When the radio goes on
To my favourite song,
I can't wait to sing like a nightingale,
That's just me!

Kimisha Hirani (11)
Copthall School

Me

There is only one of me
And nobody can replace me.

Nobody looks like I do,
Nobody has the sparkling eyes I have,
Nobody has the loving smile I have.

Nobody likes pizza like I do,
Nobody munches pizza like me,
Nobody enjoys pizza like I do.

Nobody cries like me
When I'm upset,
Nobody laughs like me
When I'm happy.

Nobody can ever be me,
I am the only one.

Forum Mehta (12)
Copthall School

This Is Me

It's me, it's me,
Like the sun in the sky,
Like a bird that's flying real high,
Totally cool as a penguin,
As peaceful as a dove,
It's me,
As graceful as a ballerina,
As pretty as a flower,
As funny as a hyena,
But sometimes I am sour.

Victoria Eldridge (11)
Copthall School

ABOUT ME!

Look at this
It's me!
It's as if the winter has broken down
And the summer has come into the big town.
I am happy as a lark,
Scared of the dark,
Cheerful in the daylight,
But without a fight.
I like dancing, gracefully like a swan
And singing like a nightingale,
Not being pale and to fail,
It's me, it's me,
Busy as a bee,
That's me!

Priyanka Agarwal (11)
Copthall School

ME!

My name is Carli
I'm young like a baby,
And free like the wind.

I'm as happy as a dolphin swimming in the sea
I'm as cheeky as a cheetah
As cunning as a fox
I'm as cold as a lion
As graceful as a swan.

Look! Look! Look!
It's me! It's me! It's me!
I'm all these, just wait and see.

Carli Langston (12)
Copthall School

Me

Just look at this, it's me,
I'm different you see,
As sly as a fox,
As steady as a rock,
As noisy as can be,
But that's just me!

Hair as dark as a winter's night,
Eyes as bright as a car's headlights,
Tall and strong as a tree,
Friendly, happy and busy.

When I'm sleeping like a bear,
All my problems, I don't care!
When I'm swimming like a fish
Or eating my favourite dish,
Climbing like a monkey in the air,
My life's a twister at the fair.

Susie Ellis (11)
Copthall School

Myself

I am tall and slim,
I always have a grin.
I love dancing and singing,
My phone at home is always ringing,
I like to fool around,
I'm always acting the clown,
At school I play netball,
Also I kick around a football,
I enjoy school, it's pretty cool.

Laura Taylor (11)
Copthall School

I And Me

Nobody looks like me.
Nobody laughs like me.
Nobody talks like me.
Nobody acts like me.
Nobody cries like me.

No one wears clothes like me.
No one eats the way I eat.
No one walks the way I walk.
No one runs the way I run.
No one smiles the way I smile.

No person draws like me.
No person paints like me.
No person writes like me.
No person reads like me.
No person spells like me.

Kasia Clinton-Carter (11)
Copthall School

Only One Of Me

There's only one of me
Nobody can get another copy
From a photocopy machine

Nobody has my looks
Nobody has my books
Nobody has my fingerprints
As there is only one of me

My mum has only one of me
And she doesn't want another copy!

Pia Gill (11)
Copthall School

Me. Emily. No One Else

There are many Emilys,
But only one of me.
There are many girls in my school,
But none know what I know.

No one knows my family the way I do,
No one knows how I feel and how sensitive I am.

There are many who know my friends,
But they don't know them the way I do.

Many can dance, but not how I dance,
Many know the songs I know,
But they don't sing with the same feeling that I do,
Many have been to the same places I've been to,
But haven't seen them the way I have.

No one can talk the way I talk,
No can walk the way I walk,
No one can smile the way I smile,
No one can laugh the way I laugh.

No one has the same hair as me
Or the same eyes as me.
No one can cry like me
Or love like me.

I am Emily. Me. Only me. No one else.

Emily Louise Curtis-Harper (11)
Copthall School

Only Me . . .

There is only one of me
And no one can be like me,
Not by disguising,
Not even by pretending
And certainly not by using a duplicating machine.

No one likes everything that I really like,
No one enjoys pizza as much as I,
No one exactly has the same skills that I do,
Not even my mum, my sister or dad.

Once I'm sad, I start moaning,
Once I'm happy, I start enjoying,
But the thing is I'm me and only me
And I will always stay different to every 'she'!

I am unique
And have my own feelings,
I like different things
And have my own belongings.

The only thing is,
If I had a twin,
She might have had the same clothes,
But never the same nose.

You see, I'm different,
What else do I bring?
I'm sure you've got it now,
I've told you everything!

Summen Hussain (11)
Copthall School

SISTERS

I have three sisters,
Imagine that.
Two older and one younger.
My two older sisters don't bother me much,
But my little sister, she's a whole different story.

Every morning, ever since she started here,
At my school, it's become a lot worse.
Every morning, she'll come to my room,
Saying, 'Rafia, Rafia' until she's nudged me enough to awaken me.
'Wake up, you need to start getting ready for school.'
Then I'll sit up and yell at her,
'Get lost, it's only 6:30am.'

One hour later, I'll get up,
Still in my PJs and there she is,
In the living room, already dressed.
Eating her Frosties, watching MTV,
I laugh and walk over to the bathroom.

Just as I'm about to do my toothpaste,
Guess who walks in? My little sister,
'Hurry up' and I scream back,
'We're not going to be late, get lost.'

At 8:00am we both walk out, not talking,
Until I have to ask her where should we meet,
Then we start talking again.

Rafia Rashid (12)
Elizabeth Garrett Anderson Girls' School

Fireworks

Boom! Bang! Sizzle! Pop!

Smoke! Screams all around
But still I couldn't hear a sound.
'World War 3' someone shouted,
Hearing those words, my heart pounded.

Boom!

A girl screamed in my ear,
From a far distance I could hear a cheer.
I searched around when another bang came
But all I could see was the absolute same.
Suddenly a smiling face appeared,
There he was, he leered
Over the fence and shouted,
'It's only fireworks!'
And disappeared.

Abiola Bello (13)
Elizabeth Garrett Anderson Girls' School

Shopping

Shoulders drooped from heavy loads
Miss Selfridge and Topshop
Lots of people crossing roads
People at the bus stop

Now it's all finished
Money's all gone
Shopping spirit diminished . . .

Maggie Young (13)
Elizabeth Garrett Anderson Girls' School

WEATHER IS NEVER JUST RIGHT!

Do you wanna be my day?
Every day we'll go and play,
The weather traps buds in May,
The summer's reign is just too short,
From time to time we say it's hot
And dull sometimes it is!
Sometimes your beauty fades,
It's nature that is changing you,
But *your* beauty will never flop,
You never ever lose a drop,
Death will never grab you,
These lines in time, will never die,
If you live on and I die,
This poem is made for you and I.

Nicole Williams (13)
Elizabeth Garrett Anderson Girls' School

TONY BUSH

The sky turned black, as if it knew,
Why they were coming, what they were going to do,
The first plane hit, everyone stopped in their tracks,
Looking around, checking their backs.
A freak accident, everyone assumed,
But when the second one hit, darkness loomed,
There was nowhere safe, nowhere to hide
And in the end it's not for us to decide.

Una Dunleavy (14)
Elizabeth Garrett Anderson Girls' School

A Friend Or Not?

Does she stick by you, through thick and thin?
Can she give a helping hand?
Does she know when you're in trouble?
Can she help you through until the end?
Is she
A friend or not?

Will she keep all secrets safe
So you have no need to worry?
Will she always be trusted
So you can be friends always and forever?
Is she
A friend or not?

Amanda Wood (14)
Elizabeth Garrett Anderson Girls' School

Feelings From Beneath My Heart!

Ever felt the feeling of a broken heart?
Ever felt the pain from beneath the scorching heart?
It's like you've broken and you've fallen apart,
Your heart cannot be put together, not even in 100 years.
Times I remember when you made me smile,
Times I remember when you made me cry,
My love for you has no secrets or boundaries,
It's all in my inner feelings,
Devouring in every pint of my blood,
Falling in love is easy, but breaking a heart is hard,
So if you once loved me, I believe I still remain in your heart!

Nazia Butt (13)
Elizabeth Garrett Anderson Girls' School

EXPECTATIONS

We have found out about us,
Head, organs, toes and all,
We haven't fully succeeded,
All we want is:

An end to cancer,
A cure for all!
No more AIDS,
Not one life will fade.

Our expectations for the millennium,
It only gave us hope,
Oh well, we won't give up!
Bring on the next millennium.

Daniella Young (13)
Elizabeth Garrett Anderson Girls' School

JAZZ

My uncle's dog loved to drink tea,
he was so full of life and energy.
It's hard to believe he's no longer here,
the thought of him still brings a tear.
He was so cheeky, funny, cute and sweet,
now he's left us, we all feel weak.
His name was Jazz as you may of guessed
and believe me, he was the best.

Charlene Ryan (14)
Elizabeth Garrett Anderson Girls' School

SUMMER'S DAY

Do u wanna be compared to a summer's day?
Na, you're too buff for that.
Although you do have your day in summer,
Summer flies quickly,
But make sure you don't.
Sometimes you're too hot to handle,
Other times you're as cold as ice,
Don't forget to put your make-up on,
Cos your spot will show through,
But that does not apply to you,
The eternal summer won't fade.

Miski Scerif (13)
Elizabeth Garrett Anderson Girls' School

WHAT ARE FRIENDS FOR?

Have you asked yourself 'What are friends for?'
Are they for the trust, love or maybe for the pain or more.
Well, once I had a friend, who I could trust but now I'm not so sure,
Looking back through the memories,
I can see that my heart was torn,
Tears were dripping which will never bring her back.
I used to tell her everything from bad things to worse,
But now I won't be able to do this,
As this is for a fact.

Mehrun Begum (14)
Elizabeth Garrett Anderson Girls' School

FRIENDS!

F riends are forever
R ude? Never!
I love them with all my heart
E ven if we fight, we never want to part!
N aughty, but my best mates,
D on't hurt them, they are great!
S pecial friends forever!

Sibel Korkmaz (14)
Elizabeth Garrett Anderson Girls' School

TO KNOW THE MEANING OF LOVE

How do I love thee?
I don't know how can I love you?
I love you from the moon to the stars,
I can feel your love, joy and your pain.
The way you look appears to my sight,
Your eyes twinkle shaped like a kite,
Bright as candlelight.
Care and affection comes deep from my heart,
I can't bear when we're apart.
I respect your faith and honesty,
My love is deep and pure.
Oh! You couldn't give me more.
Together happy with laughter and attract,
Maybe our love is a pact.
We are so free, there is no need to act.
Keeping hope and songs of good deeds,
We know how we love thee indeed.

Stephanie Tandoh (15)
La Sainte Union Convent School

Ode To My Cat

When I first saw her she was small and weak,
I decided to call her Plama,
Plama means spot in Polish
And my cat was black and white with a spot on her nose,
She was my own cat.

I loved her so,
She loved me back,
I fed her and cleaned her,
I took care of my cat,
Her fur was clean and sleek.

A few years later,
Now she's gone,
She went right over my holiday,
She left me on my own,
Plama, my own cat.

I came back from my holiday,
And went to call her name,
But I didn't hear her twinkling bell,
Or see her shining eyes,
She never came.

After a few days I got worried
And I started to drop notes under everyone's door and house,
She was found a month later,
In my neighbour's garden by their garden fence,
But my mum never let me see her body.

Every night I whisper her name
And as if in answer to my call a cat sits outside my window,
With a spot on its nose and a stripe on its tail,
I know this cat, it comes every night,
But it's not my cat.

Alice Szymankiewicz (12)
La Sainte Union Convent School

The Seasons Of Life

Summer comes and summer goes,
the days are long but sadly the night-time grows.

As the darkness leers in sight,
first the rainfall, then the streets of white.

It's so cold, I can feel it shuddering through my body,
from my ears to my nose, shooting sharply down to my toes,
sadly no one is here for me to hold.

I look on to see my skin turn pale,
the winter chill has already set sail.
Summer fun has left the air, in its place
are autumn leaves carelessly blown everywhere.

Christmas is rolling in, the bright lights are put up,
I see children with their loved ones, happily smiling, stopping to stare,
God bless them all with love and care.

My heart freezes not one beat can be heard,
as my lips turn blue I begin to get scared.

I take my last breath and close my eyes tight
and in the place of darkness I see a bright light.

As I am greeted with death he clasps my hand
and tells me not to be afraid, there is a happy place
where I shall spend the rest of my days.

Now I am an angel sent by God to watch over all
those who feel unloved.

But one thing you must remember
and please don't despair.

There will always be someone who loves you.
Why don't you try looking up there.

Kirsty Dyra (14)
La Sainte Union Convent School

GOODBYE

Here, I'll say that fatal word,
that meant so many different feelings
and reactions and reasons,
just one word.

Just seven letters
could cause so much pain
in the mortal word,
just seven letters, that's all.

I don't want to shed a tear,
I didn't want this day to come,
Though, I have to be brave,
for my sake, as well as yours.

Who knows what the future will hold,
maybe one day we'll meet again,
see the differences,
remembering the good old times.

So, here I go
with a heavy heart and tears,
I'll say that fatal word
that causes so much pain.

I'll say it, 'Goodbye,'
and may your future
bring you happiness
and success.

Elizabeth Wong (15)
La Sainte Union Convent School

Hidden Thoughts Of Dishonest Success

As I walk through the valley of pain
Troubled by confusion,
I slowly realise things shall never be the same.
Should have told the truth, rather than lie,
Mind in mayhem,
When one decides too fast, but man can only try.
Too late to apologise or remorse,
Clock still ticking,
For time is precious, yet no time to pause.
Learn from your mistakes, the proverb reads,
As many they may be.
If lesson learnt thou shall smile at one's deeds.
To succeed a goal I had to stride hard,
Do what had to be done,
Left people gutted, ashamed, scarred.
Business is booming was the talk of the day,
Taxing down, interest high,
Money making me was all my face could say.
But one cannot be sad and bitter,
Life is rich,
Therefore more green paper is good especially quicker.
I believed I was happy and lead a good life,
Blessed with wealth,
Obviously not so good as distraught carried me to the knife,
Lifestyle was perfect but living was pain,
Never had friends or love,
Only hope I could change, reality check, things shall never be the same.

Ijeoma Okoli (14)
La Sainte Union Convent School

SOMETHING I'LL NEVER FORGET

Something I'll never forget is this time that I can be free,
Opportunities all coming my way,
Mucking around dancing so wild!
Everyone is watching me from miles and miles away.
The rain gushes down while I spin around,
Has something twitched in my mind?
Is this really happening in my life?
No one would ever believe that this is me,
Gracious, shy, never telling lies, that's what everyone thinks I am.

I've never thought I'd ever be like this,
Living my life freely,
Lively, yes me!

Never knew things like these could be so special,
Every day I want to do this,
Vivacious character that's what I now have,
Every individual needs to do this,
Realise how special life actually is.

Forgetting all those troubles in my mind,
Overwhelmed, that's how I feel,
Realising love is in the air that we breathe,
Grateful for the freedom that's all over my body, that's I,
Everybody watching is much better than none,
Thinking about my time in this life, I've been grateful, loving and kind
And now I've used the freedom from my mind.

Mary-Grace Sturley (12)
La Sainte Union Convent School

THE DREAM

I watched a giant butterfly
With wings of coloured glass
Come flying through the window
Of my afternoon English class.
It carried precious cargo
Of three sailors from the moon
Hoping that they would get to sea
To sail very soon.
Each sailor carried a fuzzy cloud
That was made of magenta floss
Encased in a furry basket
Constructed of emerald moss.
'Would you care to join us?'
They all said as one.
'We can bounce between the stars
And go swimming on the sun.
We'll take you to a funny place
Where the spongy ground shoots up rain,
Where the pale clouds are sprouting branches
And yellow bricks make up the lane.'
Though it sounded like great fun,
I decided to stay,
But there were no hard feelings
So they all went on their way.
I heard a final call farewell
With the sound of joyous laughter,
All that I can hope for them
Is that they lived happily ever after.

Then suddenly, the school bell rang
Rousing me from my sleep,
When I saw my teacher's face
I thought I was in trouble deep.
But she gave me a kindly smile
(Or so it seemed)
Then told me to write a poem
All about my dream.

Susan Marmito (13)
La Sainte Union Convent School

The Mysterious Trousers

You would not believe the grief my trousers gave
One summer.

They disappeared forever.
One summer.

I went to pack my bag
One summer

I searched high and low
One summer

No trousers ever that do better than them
One summer

Gone.

Kirsten Vass (14)
La Sainte Union Convent School

Lonely

Alone I shall walk
Alone I shall bear my soul
Alone my grievance carries
Alone my heart be still.

I am lonely for I have no shepherd
I have no song
I have no life
I am alone for I am unique
I am but one of a kind
I am but me

I am alone in spirit, in soul
But I am needed in mind
I am needed but I am not wanted
I am alone for my heart begs it

Lonely I am
Lonely I have become
Lonely I remain.

Eva Nyandoro (15)
La Sainte Union Convent School

My Views On Life

When you're alone and you suddenly feel a slight
Cold breeze brush up against you,
People say you're in the presence of a ghost
And when you're with friends and it suddenly goes quiet,
Angels go by, but who knows.
Breathe and live,

Live and breathe,
Do not breathe then die,
Do breathe and live,
Live life to the fullest
Or die alone.

Mary Ezekiel (15)
La Sainte Union Convent School

THE GHETTOS

The ghettos in Poland were a tearful sight,
Crying all day, crying all night.
Children and adults swollen with hunger,
Isolated, taken under.
Without clothing, without shoes,
Only skeletons walk.
Adults and children dying every day,
I only wish there was something to say.
Vicious Germans walking around,
They're happy they did this,
Pushing them to the ground.
'Decaying and rotten,'
They always say,
Looking at them in disgust every day.
Ghetto coach trips is their main attraction,
Reducing the Jews to a very small fraction.
A young Jewish boy begging in the streets,
Nothing upon his own two feet.
A little skeleton,
Sunken eyes,
He hates the Nazis, he's despised.
Barely anything to eat or drink,
I hope this poem makes people think.

Nicola Tozzi (11)
La Sainte Union Convent School

Enigma

When the pearly gates of Heaven open up,
who will be there to tell me it's real?
When the day comes when my mum dies,
who will be there to tell me why?
When the world collapses around me,
who will be there to tell me why it's now?
When I meet the love of my life,
who will be there to tell me how?

When the future is the present,
who will be there to tell me what the future is?
When men fly in space,
who will be there to tell me what was wrong with Earth?
When the cure for cancer is discovered,
who will be there to tell me how it originates?
Why are there so many questions
and so little who ask them?

What is the meaning of life?

Zina Wegrzynski (12)
La Sainte Union Convent School

Symphony Of Bittersweet

My heart wept bitterly,
Through the darkest, coldest night I ever saw.
Like a mermaid, I waited eternally,
For your ship to sail ashore.

Teardrops from my eyes cascaded
And as a lonesome unicorn I wandered.
In the deepest ocean, I drowned
And on the highest mountain, I pondered.

I looked in my deepest memories,
When those graceful nights could not be ours.
A shadow appeared in the distance, saying,
'Close your eyes and meet me in the stars.'

I continue to cry my melodious call,
On my stone, all night and day.
My call, a symphony of bittersweet,
To end this torture, I pray.

Samantha Montes Otalvaro (16)
La Sainte Union Convent School

MOMENTS WHICH DEFINE US

It was the hardest thing I had to face
All feelings of self worth had gone
All that was left was a hollow space
There felt no point in going on

That's when you came along
Made me see that life went on
You never gave up, you saw it through
What did I do to deserve you?

Most left, a few stayed
True friends you will remain
Those that didn't - no hate is there
What stopped you was fear

I understand.

Sharon Donovan (15)
La Sainte Union Convent School

THE PLACE I CALL HOME

Home smells sweet like sugar
Home is as warm as a dream
When I go out of my home
The warmth shatters
Like glass
Sharp and cold
Just like ice
So cold it cuts into my hands
Like a hundred razors
All of a sudden
I start tingling
Until I go numb
It feels like my skin is bubbling
And my hair is standing on end
I take a step forward
I step in a puddle
Stones and damp
Swimming around in my shoe
I try to look up
A drop in my eye
The rain begins to pour
I shiver . . .
But I continue . . .

Vanessa Adams (11)
Mount Carmel School for Girls

HELL

Danger was coming with the bubbling lava,
Dripping down making a stream,
Fireballs blazing up in the air,
Down came the dripping lava,
Devils appearing as the sun went down,
Smiling with a big fat grin,

Coming towards me a big red man,
Laughing as loud as a banging drum,
Down came the dripping lava,
The big red flames rising very high in the sky,
The sky's turning red.

Cassandra Batchelor (11)
Mount Carmel School for Girls

REST IN PEACE AMERICA - 11TH SEPTEMBER 2001

God looked around his garden and saw an empty space,
Then looking down from Heaven he saw America's loving face,
He wrapped his arms around them,
Told them to come to rest,
His garden must be beautiful because he only takes the best,
If tears could build a stairway,
Memories a lane,
I would climb up to Heaven to see the people of America again,
We think of you in silence,
We even speak your names,
But all that is left is in memory
And pictures in a frame,
Rest in peace all those people that have died,
Every passing day families have cried,
We miss you America,
We really do,
Keep in loving memory,
We're praying for you.

Rest in peace all those innocent people
Who have sadly passed away on
Tuesday 11th September 2001.

Forever in our hearts, dreams and prayers.

Margaret Fitzgerald (14)
Mount Carmel School for Girls

My Brothers

My brothers are annoying
They make me go crazy, they are younger than me
What should I do?
Someone has to help me, I don't know what to do,
I love to send them upstairs and tell them off too
I tell them to go away and scream at them too
And tell them what to do
I have to help my brothers sometimes
Shout at them too, God please help me,
I'll pray to you, if that is what I have to do to stop them
And lock them up in their room
I play my music very loud
So I can't hear them
I sometimes wish that
I had a lock on my door
So I can lock them out
Won't anyone please help me?

Channé Telford (11)
Mount Carmel School for Girls

Silence

The deadly silence was deafening
I felt a chill climbing up my spine
What's about to happen?
My stomach began to whine
My feet started moving
But I was standing still
What's about to happen?
I couldn't even squeal

The ground started splitting
Like my mouth, opening wide
My body just standing still
Like a block of ice
Then the ground just closed again
And left me with only silence
Was I dreaming? Was it real
Or was it nature making a deal?

Tonie Julianna Marciano (11)
Mount Carmel School for Girls

CREEPY CASTLE

There are grey clouds,
I shout out loud.
Closing walls are hurting me.
The room is dark,
Statues are everywhere.
The servants are looking at me.
Storms, thunder and big frames are creepy.
What was that?
Laughter came from under!
Ghosts are playing.
As I lie down,
Suddenly swords, knives and axes fly up in the air.
The room is cold,
I feel a chill in my spine!
I am so scared I think my death
Is coming!

Giovanna Gutierrez Torres (12)
Mount Carmel School for Girls

THE BURGLARS

I woke up one evening,
Heard thumping downstairs,
I crept out of bed, cuddling my bears.
Who could it be?
I peered round the corner,
I only wished I found out sooner,
A fat, plump man and a skinny one too,
Standing in the kitchen,
I wondered what to do.
My foot slipped,
Making a terrible sound.
I tumbled down the stairs
And fell to the ground.
These gruesome men
Carrying big, black sacks,
Which they tried to hide behind their backs,
Stumbled over, glared at me then yelled to each other,
'Who on earth is she?'
My dad leapt out of bed,
'What's going on?' my mother said.
'There's a noise downstairs,
No need to worry,
There's two men down there who will wish they were sorry.'
My mother dialled 999,
Hoping that the police would make it in time.
Unfortunately my dad tripped over the hoover
And in no time at all they made a quick manoeuvre,
The police had finally arrived
With both the burglars side by side.

'Back to bed,' my father said.
For the rest of the night I slept with my mother,
She kissed my cheek and hugged my brother.
My dad squeezed in and held us tight
And yawned, 'It's been a very long night.'

Philippa Atkinson (11)
Palmers Green High School

The African Beat

The African drums swing into a steady beat
The leopard, handsome and elegant
Awakes from his lair,
His ears twitch and his eyes gleam,
The drums beat faster every second,
The leopard races across the plain,
His blood pounding and his muscles pumping

And he pounces
And the drums stop beating
He bites into the deer's neck,
Blood gushes out of the wound,
The job is done,
The music finished.

The leopard lays content among the rocks,
The night drifts in with its stars and moon,
The African sun with its golden beams,
Fades away into the distance,
The cool breeze
Mops the leopard's brow,
The day is over,
The sun gone down.

Sacha Kreeger (10)
Palmers Green High School

THE GHOST OF JACOB MARLEY 'DREADFUL APPARITION WHY DO YOU TROUBLE ME'

A freezing, foggy eventide,
Seven years to the night that Marley died,
Scrooge arrived at Marley's edifice,
Marley though dead, deep down was sorely missed,
As Scrooge as usual reached for the door,
He glanced at a sight, which chilled him to the core.

A sight so ghostly, the colour so foul,
The winds blew round him with whistles and yowls,
A face so familiar, yet a face so unknown,
A face of a friend, a face of a foe,
Scrooge looked away and blinked his eyes,
And thought that his mind was telling lies.

Scrooge entered his chambers with fear in his mind,
His troubled, fearful face was lined,
He thought he saw a hearse on the stair,
But he knew that it could not really be there,
The bells began to softly swing,
Within minutes it turned into a deafening ring.

He heard the clank of chains below him,
The fire in the grate flickered and became dim,
The cellar door flung open with a crash,
And coming up the stairs he heard the chains lash,
The fire leapt up as if to shout,
I know him, Marley's ghost, get out!

Marley's appearance was exactly the same,
But he was transparent for which himself he did blame,
He was a paragon of unhappiness, a ghost full of woe,
A ghost who never stops, a ghost who never slows,
Jacob Marley was a friend indeed that night,
For he warned Scrooge of his terrible plight.

Laura Coyne (12) & Bryony Hirsch (13)
Palmers Green High School

MOONLIGHT

Liquid silver
Pouring in silent, quivering waves,
Softly over the velvet night.
Gently shimmering folds
Of fine, floating gauze,
Drifting down from the black silk
Of the star-bejewelled sky,
Casting its quiet enchantment
Over the sleeping world.

Chloë Brown (12)
Palmers Green High School

THE LADY OF DORSET

There once was a lady of Dorset,
She unfortunately died from a corset,
It was tied up too tight,
So she died in the night,
That poor old lady of Dorset.

Raphaella Mazaheri-Asadi (11)
Palmers Green High School

Tick-Tock

Tick-tock, tick-tock,
I'm meant to be writing a letter,
To tell Lisa we hope she feels better,
But no ideas come to mind,
A good one I'll never find.

Tick-tock, tick-tock,
The time is passing fast,
Maybe I'll copy something from the past,
No! That's a ridiculous idea,
Should I ask Auntie Maria?

Tick-tock, tick-tock,
I still haven't written a word,
This is just absurd,
Why do I have to write this horrid letter,
She'll soon phone and say she's better.

Tick-tock, tick-tock,
I think I'm going to explode,
My head is bursting, *overload!*
I am no longer grinning from ear to ear,
This is a nightmare, right here.

Tick-tock, tick-tock,
Anyway, let's get back to this wretched thing,
Oh, that's the phone, bring, bring,
'Finally Mum, you're off the phone,
That was Lisa, wasn't it? I could tell by your tone.'

Tick-tock, tick-tock,
'Yes dear it was,' Mum finally replied.
Then I started to sob, I just cried and cried,
'Did she say she was better?'
'Yes dear, now you don't have to write that letter.'

Shivani Jethwa (11)
Palmers Green High School

School Is Cool!

School is cool,
School is great.
We have to be there,
At half-past eight.

School is cool,
School is wicked,
Especially if
You're a bright kid.

School is cool,
School is brilliant,
We do music
And we learn to chant.

School is cool,
School is fun,
We love to go, although
Our bags weigh a ton.

School is cool,
School is enjoyable,
We learn to be strong,
So wise and so able.

School is cool,
School is paradise,
Science and labs,
We get to be precise.

Zahra Roberts (11)
Palmers Green High School

THE TIGER

With its variegated pattern,
Shows off with its vibrant colours,
As it prances through lush vegetation,
Sensing its vicious world around it.

Its eyes are shocking amber,
Those broad amazing whiskers,
The stabbing of jaws are fearful,
'Twas the king of cats and the jungle,
As its whole body stands out with grace and beauty.

It gazes at the rustle in the undergrowth,
It quietly sauntered its way,
A deer peacefully devoured its food,
Within less than a second the tiger had
Leapt up into the air
And dropped dead,
A life lost from its powerful body,
A spotted rug lies in a room, in the city.

Rencis Baletti (11)
Palmers Green High School

THE EAGLE

The eagle soars over the dusty moors,
The animals quickly hide from this cause.

The eagle gently glides up so high,
He watches closely as he passes by.

The eagle searches for his food,
He is in the hunting mood.

The eagle rustles his fine wings,
For he knows that he is king.

Nicole Fredman (11)
Palmers Green High School

THE NEW YORK DISASTER!

The hunt for survivors still goes on,
The adults and children lie upon
The masses of concrete, steel and rubble,
Terrorists are now in big trouble.
The trade twin towers have fallen down,
New York has lost its highest crown.
Two planes crashed in and people died,
Survivors stood and looked and cried.
The Pentagon was also hit,
The fire burned for hours, lit.
20 thousand people expected dead,
We all don't know what lies ahead.
The human missiles used for war,
An awful sight not seen before.
It must be stopped, this has to end!
The cities people all will mend.
The towers will be built once more,
But other buildings on the floor.

We should all say a prayer,
For the thousands who will lay there!

Louise Jane Currie (12)
St Mary's CE High School, Downage

FINAL DAWN

The sun is shining,
A day wind blows,
The dust rises
And settles in the young child's mouth.

He runs to his mother,
His huge eyes
Begging for food,
The mother shakes her head,
Signalling, no.

The child's bony form
Racks with sobs.
It's been this way for
Many weeks now.
Waking without food
And sleeping without food.

Every day, we watch as
The sun rises,
Every day we watch
The sun set.

We count the days,
As they drag by
And we ask
'O Lord! What have we done
To anger you as every day
Seems like a final dawn.

Salma Bashir (12)
St Mary's CE High School, Downage

TWEETY PIE

Me and my Tweety Pie
He never tells me any lies
He sits on my bed
With the pillow under his head
Waiting for me to come home from school
Lying there thinking he's cool
Me and Tweety are best of friends
Whenever there's a problem we always make amend
I love my Tweety
He loves me too
One day, Tweety, we'll have to depart
But you'll always be in my heart
Me and my Tweety Pie.

Michelle Brown (12)
St Mary's CE High School, Downage

STRANGE MAN

One day, I was walking down to town,
To buy myself a dressing gown,
As I walked down my long, long street,
To my surprise; a stranger to meet,
I looked at his pale eyes and long black hair
And he looked back with a scary stare.
I tried to move but my legs were stiff,
I woke up suddenly all cold and blue,
Trying to find out if this dream was really true,
I never saw that man when I was all alone,
Wondering about with no home,
I pray for that man every day,
Hoping he will find a place to stay.

Geraldin Vassell (13)
St Mary's CE High School, Downage

A Mother's Day Poem
(Dedicated to my mum)

Before you start
This was a part
Of a present
For my mummy

Mummy, I love you
Mummy, I do
All of these gifts are just for you

I hope you enjoy this Mother's Day
And beg to yourself
Please don't go away
But never forget, it'll come back next year
I'm sorry for moaning
Please don't have a beer

There's one more thing I'd like to add
You're my mum
And well, I'm glad.

Julie Anne King (12)
St Mary's CE High School, Downage

My Best Friend

I thank God every day
    for a friend like you
Someone I can confide
    my joys and sorrows to
Someone who doesn't judge me
    whatever I do
Thank God for a friend like you . . .

I thank God every day
    for a friend like you
Someone who is there
    whenever I'm blue
Someone who I could talk to
    all day through
Thank God for a friend like you.

Koel Mathur (13)
St Mary's CE High School, Downage

SPORTS

Sports
All different types of sports
Football, cricket, tennis
Kicking the ball
Hitting the ball
Throwing the ball
Many sports you can play
Always entertaining you

Playing sport is great fun
Golf, swimming, hockey
Using a stick
Kicking your left
Or swinging your arm
Many sports you may like
Join a club
At your school
Or somewhere near your house
All different types of sports!

Taufiq Daroge (12)
St Mary's CE High School, Downage

My Teddy Bear

I've had this bear,
I've given it care,
For years and years and years.

It had a mare,
But it's lost its hair,
For years and years and years.

While I was making the bed,
Out popped its head
And now you can see the fluff
And to my mum I have to bluff,
For years and years and years.

Then came the ear,
And now it can't hear,
For years and years and years.

Out came an eye
And now it can't cry,
For years and years and years.

My teddy bear is very sad
Because I've been bad,
Very bad to it
And now all it can do is sit,
For years and years and years.

Meera P Soni (12)
St Mary's CE High School, Downage

Horror Time

A chill down your spine,
Oh yeah, it's horror time.
A click and a clack,
Silence then dark.

Now it's coming closer,
Just round the corner.
A claw on your shoulder, *boo!*
Too late, it's got you.

Cynthia Seda (12)
St Mary's CE High School, Downage

Attack On America

On the day that it happened,
A day people will not forget,
A day of terrorism,
A day of nightmares,
A day of death,
A day of crying,
A day of loneliness.

Who did it?

André Loh (12)
St Mary's CE High School, Downage

Autumn Is Here

Autumn is here,
Autumn is here,
The leaves are falling,
Leaving the trees bare.
Do you see the wind in the air
Rushing and rushing, bringing autumn here?

Sharon Ngetich (12)
St Mary's CE High School, Downage

Our Sun

Golden, like a gleaming medal
Hung round one's neck
Blazing, scorching
Like petrol being lit, metal melting.

Bringer of swimsuits
Bright blue beach towels
Beads of sweat, laughter
Evening begins, pastel pinks, reds filling skies.

The sun disappears
To warm another day
It reappears to spread more smiles
And to share more glory.

The sun, mighty
Everyone's amazing companion
The light and life of the world.

Natalie Welch (12)
St Mary's CE High School, Downage

Horror Is Sweet

Kids beware
Horror is scary
You're in for a scare
Monsters are hairy

Houses are dark
People raise from the dead
Zombie dogs bark
From right under your bed

Lightning flashing
Thunder appeared
Cars crashing
People are scared

People dying
Boo
Vampires flying
Will scare you.

Darius Neil (12)
St Mary's CE High School, Downage

Shooting Star

Shooting star, I gaze at you
Because I know he loved them too

Shared memories, now far apart
Are a whistling wind inside my heart

Laughter, jokes and fantasy
Are kept in bubbles inside me

While worries, tears and scowls and frowns
Are a red hot flame burning deep down

Ideals and shared hopes and dreams
Gone forever, ripped at seams

It's a miracle star, down from above
But what's the point of marvelling without someone you love?

Helen Downer (12)
St Mary's CE High School, Downage

LIFE

Life is long
Like a song
Sometimes Scot likes my sport
Life's a pong
Like my bong
Sometimes short
Like Uncle's snort
Life's mysterious
Like Miss Serious
Sometimes boring
Like Uncle snoring
Life is fun
Like a bun
Sometimes sad
With something bad

Oh life, life
I enjoyed my life
Thanks to my wife
My life is gone
Thanks to John
Well, I guess you can say it's life.

Brigitte King Mlotshwa (12)
St Mary's CE High School, Downage

ICE

It sends a chill down your spine,
Your body feels like lime.
The white all around us,
None of it making a sound.

There's a snowman in the distance,
All wrapped up tight and warm.
Ice, ice, extremely cold,
Will always be alone.

Kyle Roberts (13)
St Mary's CE High School, Downage

AUTUMN

Autumn time, autumn time,
Brand new trees and little leaves,
All fall down.

Autumn is a time when leaves are all colours,
Green, yellow and brown,
Covering the ground.

Children playing,
Picking leaves,
Watching them come down
To rest again.

Autumn is here,
Over and over again,
Never been missed
By cheerful faces
And people pacing
To the leaves.

But autumn has to end sometime.

Bernice Amissah (12)
St Mary's CE High School, Downage

WHAT IS A CAT?

A kitten is a baby,
Its eyes just start to open,
It claws start to scratch,
Its eyes open, it sees the world.

When the cat gets older,
It starts to see things,
People and other cats,
Its eyes are looking at you like a lost cat,
Its claws are like sharp knives,
Going to scratch you,
When the cat gets angry
Its tail swings around,
Like a child playing on a swing.

Chantal Crosby (12)
St Mary's CE High School, Downage

SCHOOL! SCHOOL! SCHOOL!

Everyone seems so mean
When you just join school
The teachers seem so nice, it is a dream
When you just join school
You try to make some mates
When you just join school
Now I am in year eight
I saw the year sevens
They looked scared
On the first day of school
But now they try to act all big and cool
School, school, school.

Aisha Adesanya (12)
St Mary's CE High School, Downage

A Wonderful World

Have you ever seen the sunrise as it shines
the sky with light, or felt a gentle breeze
go by that made you want to fly?
Have you ever seen a waterfall
and listened to its sound?
Have you ever seen a shining star
shoot across the sky?
Have you ever felt a snowflake fall
onto your hand?
Have you ever seen the ocean as it
crashes onto the sand or ever heard
the birds above fill the sky with music?
The Earth is full of wonder made
for you and I.

Veronica Gwembere (12)
St Mary's CE High School, Downage

True Feelings

My true feelings are deep and gloom,
Sweeping around like a prickly broom,
Sometimes I'm happy, sometimes I'm down,
But there's one special person who gets me around,
He's sweet, funny and full of love,
He's my prince charming who was sent from above,
That's my true feelings,
Thankful that it's being read
Everyone has a true feeling
Just thankful mine has spread.

Denise Ramasar-Northover (13)
St Mary's CE High School, Downage

The Millipede

The millipede is a silent train,
Moving, turning, curving,
Amongst hills and valleys,
Twigs and grass.

Moving its long segmented body,
To the rhythm that the legs set,
Using their antennae like lights,
To feel their way through the land.

Tunnelling their flat carriage-like bodies,
Under stones and mountains,
So quick, so quiet, so silent
Is the millipede.

William Hayman (12)
St Mary's CE High School, Downage

Animals

My cat is nice and soft,
Who always sleeps up in the loft.
Its name is Lin
And it always goes down the bin
And ends up covered in moths.

My dog is small and cute,
My mum says it's a brute!
What's that?
Is it a bat, rat or cat?
He's so small, he looks like a newt.

Leisha Bloomfield (12)
St Mary's CE High School, Downage

MY SPECIAL POEM

I wondered what poem I should write,
I thought I might
Talk about stars at night.

I changed my mind
Just in time,
I'm sort of in rhyme,
Do you like lime?

I like miming
In time,
Unlike this,
This is just total
Bliss!

Kirsten Moore (12)
St Mary's CE High School, Downage

ALL ALONE

The rain thudding on the tin roof
Wind howling loudly, lightning flashing
Running round the house
Looking for a torch as the lights are out

Floorboards creaking
Distant voices heard
Snuggled up in one corner whimpering
Terrified
As the door opens a disfigured creatures walks through
My dog!

Vivek Vijayakumar (12)
St Mary's CE High School, Downage

HORROR POEM

Spirits force into your bodies,
Controlling you to murder somebody,
Up and down they fly,
Wanting everyone to die.

Run, run, you're gonna die,
Under the unknown graveyard you lie,
Quick, quick, they dig into your neck,
I bet you won't guess what will happen in a sec.

Skull-crushing gremlins peep out at night,
Looking for a victim to give it a bite,
The eye-sucking skulls come out at night,
Injecting your eyeballs, getting you ready for a fright.

Naynesh Patel (13)
St Mary's CE High School, Downage

FRIENDS!

Friends are caring,
Friends are a joke,
Friends laugh at everything, even the Pope,
Friends can be jealous,
Friends can be sad,
Friends can even drive you insane or mad,
Friends can be happy,
Friends can be grim,
Friends are important, so let's all begin.

Tasmin Lewis (12)
St Mary's CE High School, Downage

PEACE! WHAT DOES IT MEAN?

If peace could be anywhere, any place, where would it be?
This word peace, what does it mean?
People say we should have peace in this world
But what does it mean?
Priests say, 'Peace be with you and go in peace'
But what does this word mean?
You hear on the news, war has stopped,
There is peace, but what does it mean?
I think this word peace is a sign or a symbol
That says everyone is happy and well,
But that's not what it means at all,
It means that this world may never be happy again,
But we can try and be happy in this sad and cruel world.

Loretta Campbell (12)
St Mary's CE High School, Downage

BASKETBALL

Basketball is my favourite sport
And I'm one of the best players on the court.
Michael Jordan, one of the best players ever,
Don't contest his shot, don't even bother.
You turn behind and the whistle blows,
He knows what it means, he knows.
You hear the ball go through the net,
You feel your body, it's wet with sweat.
You run to the ball and slam it on the floor
And this is why basketball is a sport that I adore.

Arron Keith Warmann (12)
St Mary's CE High School, Downage

POND LIFE

Sparkling water,
Beautiful birds,
Such lovely sounds,
Have you ever heard?
Birds hunting, birds flying,
Newborn babies trying, trying.
See birds flying in the sky,
Gliding like an aeroplane in the sky.
See the frogs, green and happy,
Jumping up and down like a crazy kangaroo.
See the ripples in the pond lasting forever,
Like the slight breeze around the pond.
See the beautiful colours,
Like an undiscovered, everlasting rainbow.

Leeann Bushell (12)
St Mary's CE High School, Downage

TRAGEDY IN AMERICA

It was early in the morning at 9:00am,
The loud noise of the low aeroplanes
Taking over the sky, got people worried.
Before anyone could blink, the aeroplane hit
The tower, almost going through,
The second one flew down like a bird
Falling off a tree,
Meanwhile in Washington, an aeroplane flying
300mph hit the corner of Washington's landmark,
Leaving hundreds dead.
Now things in America would never be the same again.

Sofodis Patalosarius (12)
St Mary's CE High School, Downage

THINGS I LIKE, BUT . . .

I like cheese,
but only on pizza.
I like sports,
but only when I watch it.
I like parties,
but only when I'm dancing.
I like school,
but only at break times.
I like science,
but only when it's finished.
I like theme parks,
but only the big rides.
I like films,
but only the scary films.
I like gum,
but only the cherry flavour.

Laurette Bailey (12)
St Mary's CE High School, Downage

MY BIRTHDAY

The pain of waiting for the adrenalin running
through my body for the first time of my life.
Day by day like the temptation is about to kill me.
So I feel like I just want to get it over and down with,
but when the day comes, I don't want it to end.

Samuel Omezie (11)
St Mary's CE High School, Downage

MATHS

As we think, maths is our next lesson,
Once the bell goes, we all go to *maths!*
All the lovely numbers, 1, 2, 3 and 4
We think, should we add or subtract?

As our teacher says 'Listen up,
We are going to have a test,'
Hmmm . . . we think will it be hard or will it be easy?
Do I know all what we have learnt?
'Put your pens down' the teacher will say like my mum.

When we get our results we wish that we did better,
When we finish, we will say 'I've learnt so much today.'

Meenal Khetani (11)
St Mary's CE High School, Downage

DOLPHINS

Dolphins, they can be big, they can be small,
they can be kind and friendly, they can be angry.
Dolphins eat different kinds of fish,
they drink water and they live in different places in their own schools.
They make beautiful sounds over and under,
they try and talk to you, they make you understand.
They want you to play with them, feed them, follow them.
They come to you when something has happened,
they also come when something hasn't.
Even if they've been gone for ages, they will always come back,
they'll jump and leap like you've never seen before.

Jinita Doshi (11)
St Mary's CE High School, Downage

STAR SIGN

I am Cancer,
My birthday's on 24th June,
My brother died
On the 24th June,
My brother was Cancer too
And my brother could sing too,
He could sing in his head,
I was kind to my brother,
Called Glen Edward Russell Harkness,
Cancer!
Cancer!
Cancer!

John Harkness (15)
Swiss Cottage Special School

ZODIAC

The sky is red in my heart.
The waterfall is the sunlight.
The love of moonlight is I.

Come and walk with me in the wind.
Come into the sunlight with me.
Come into the waterfall in my heart.
Come and see the scorpion in the snow and in me,
So it is for me and the world and the star signs.

Michael Hagan (15)
Swiss Cottage Special School

TAURUS

Taureans are sweet
Taureans are kind
Taureans help you out
Taureans speak their mind
Taureans say if you're fat
Taureans say if you're thin
Taureans are not fools
Taureans are the kings

All of us
Geminis, why, oh why?
Librans, why cry?
Virgos, why be so rude?
Pisces, why be fools?
Sagittarius, why try to speak your mind?
Capricorns are like flies
Leos roar as loud as you can
But don't forget Taureans are the kings
Aquarians, I look at your eyes
Cancer, I'm in disguise
Scorpians, I have run a mile
Arians, I have to go.

Toni McMorrow (15)
Swiss Cottage Special School

FIREWORK DISPLAY

Fantastic, flattering, fabulous fireworks.
Wonderful, stunning arrays flashing through the sky.
Babies crying, children laughing.
Popcorn popping, burgers and chips on the menu.

Sparks of rainbow colours in the air.
Bangers go off leaving a stench behind.
Sparklers shine in different colours.
Catherine wheels spinning away on wooden posts.

Priya Patel (11)
The Swaminarayan School

DETENTION

Getting in detention is plain torture,
You just have to hate it,
When that happens to you.
Your mind gets all stressed
And you wish you could just walk out of it.
You'd rather be having much more fun with your mates,
Than being in detention.
You'd be standing there alone,
No one to talk to and nothing to do.
Sometimes you would be in detention,
For your own friend's naughty deed.
You would just hate for that to happen
And wish they would get in trouble themselves.
Sometimes you would get in detention,
For just a little thing.
I mean, chewing gum or saying something wrong,
What's wrong with that?
Wouldn't you just hate that?
I mean, why detention?
So many questions.
Why . . .?

Heenal Patel (10)
The Swaminarayan School

Rain, Rain

Rain, rain,
The grey clouds begin to take over the blue skies,
The first raindrop falls, then the other.
Tap, tap on the concrete floor,
They come down as a small speeding fireball,
Hit the floor and then turn into a million pieces,
Then the sky begins to pour down like a leaking tap,
Rain, rain.

Rain, rain,
As the rain falls it is like a million droplets a second,
Suddenly a bright blinding light appears in the sky,
Rumble, rumble goes the thunder as the ground shakes at the same time,
After a few hours the rain stops, the sun comes out,
The concrete floor looks like plastic as the sun shines upon it,
Then in the sky there is a beautiful multicoloured rainbow
With the sun's rays penetrating through each colour,
Rain, rain.

Jaimin Thakore (13)
The Swaminarayan School

Vehicles

(Dedicated to my younger brother who's mad about cars!)

Watch that Lamborghini speeding over a hump,
Watch that Lamborghini ending up in a dump.

Off goes a Porsche,
While a Beetle is still starting.

The Porsche has a gleaming body,
Where a Mercedes has style.

Motorbikes go off in a roar
And Ferraris soar off smoothly.

A BMW has a superb interior
And a TGV is superior.

Jiten Harsiani (13)
The Swaminarayan School

TRAGEDY

Tragedy strikes New York
Twin Towers reduced to rubble
Tragedy strikes Washington
Five-sided Pentagon partly demolished

Planes hijacked
People terrorised
What insanity
What a tragedy

Fire rages out of control
Plumes of smoke bellow out
Rescuers tried to save
But concrete towers just gave

Testing time for humanity
What a waste of innocent lives
Who, with a human heart
Could do this terrible deed

Cowards will be unmasked
Justice will prevail
Have faith
It will not fail us
What a tragedy.

Bhavni Shah (12)
The Swaminarayan School

THE SEA

Swishing, swashing fearful sea,
All the noise scares me,
Mostly happy, sometimes sad,
Some tourists think that you are bad,
Crashing on icebergs and rocks,
Your deep down secrets have keys but not any locks.

Your mighty arms hold amazing creatures,
Each one has amazing features,
We pull things out of your mighty grip,
Like wrecked boats and ships,
Like a star you sparkle under the moon,
That is your extra-special boon.

All through the day,
The little children play,
They discover the hidden secrets,
But you have never any regrets,
They love you so much,
You can never remember as such!

Anushree Jagadambe (13)
The Swaminarayan School

DEEP FOREST

Deep in the forest
From whom is this so loud wail?
Deep and deep we go
Hear the deafening sound of the river flow

Forest as dark and the moon as bright
Why do I feel something so frightful?
Like the wolves and his gang howling in the wild
My hands and feet shaking violently

The night leaves my body's shadow
Like how to get out of this forest so frightening and hallow
I'm frightened, I'm scared but I don't know where to go
But I pray to God where my trail will show.

Vikunj Modha (12)
The Swaminarayan School

THE OZONE LAYER

The ozone layer in the sky,
We can't see it but it's there.
Our guardian from the sun,
Protecting us from harmful rays.

Serving us night and day,
Even though we kill it.
It serves with all its dignity,
With no expectation of something back.

The ozone layer in the sky,
Lived through history,
From Stone Age to Middle Age to World War I and II,
It has seen everything!

But soon, we say goodbye to our protector,
Because we refuse to stop polluting with our evil toxins
And gases.

We spray, we abuse, we pollute,
We say goodbye as it slowly
Withers away leaving us to wither
In its trail, leaving the world with some peace
Without any existence on it
Just left, abandoned . . .

Vikash Popat (13)
The Swaminarayan School

The Deep Blue Sea

Have you ever thought
Of visiting the deep blue sea?
No, why don't you go and have a peep?

I must go down to the deep blue sea,
To the lonely sea,
I'll go in my tall ship
And catch sight of the colourful fish
And don't forget the dolphins.

I'll observe the white, fair, charming seagulls,
As I have a jolly swim with the joyful kids.
I'll rest in the sun looking up
At the clear, blue sky,
And wonder - why didn't I ever visit
The deep blue sea?

Finally as the sun goes down,
I'll trot . . . back to my sweet home.
I'll forever remember the deep blue sea.

Meera Patel (12)
The Swaminarayan School

Pollution

Pollution makes the air full of smoke,
Instead of cars, why don't they use bicycles?
Because we need the air to be pure and cleaner
And let the Earth live on for longer.

Pollution destroys many things,
When people don't care a bit,
With rubbish thrown everywhere,
The Earth is getting filthier.

Pollution is increasing day by day,
Why don't people understand?
When pollution completely takes over,
They'll be none of us.

Ravi Kukadia (12)
The Swaminarayan School

SPIDERS

Spiders, spiders, oh brown spiders,
Why are you so scary?
Spiders, spiders, oh brown spiders,
Why are you so hairy?

Spiders, spiders, oh hairy spiders,
How do you walk so fast?
Spiders, spiders, oh hairy spiders,
Why do you make me feel so funny?

Spiders, spiders, oh brown spiders,
Why is your skin so furry?
Spiders, spiders, oh brown spiders,
Why are you brown?

Spiders, spiders, oh hairy spiders,
Why are you so ugly?
Spiders, spiders, oh hairy spiders,
How do you crawl up people?

Spiders, spiders, oh brown spiders,
Why are you so scary?
Spiders, spiders, oh brown spiders,
Why do you bring people *fear?*

Chandni Patel (12)
The Swaminarayan School

NATURE

Birds go and make their nests
And rivers flow towards the west
Trees are greener than ever before
And the grass hadn't looked better than on the open moor
Mountains and cliffs are at their highest peak
And eagles feed with their beaks
Water sparkles in the light
And rabbits hop till they're out of sight
The squirrel nibbles away
As the sun sets for another day
At night the fox is out for meat
While most of the animals sleep
There is a low, cool breeze
And everything's at ease
Back in the morning the sun is bright
And everybody's out to play in the light
Birds start to sing
Animals start to bring
Food for their young
As the day has begun.

Sagar Patel (12)
The Swaminarayan School

I LOOKED INTO THE DARK SKY

I looked into the dark sky
And saw something fly high
What it was, I didn't know
Just then the wind gave me a mighty blow

As it came near
I saw a shadow appear
Just then I realised
It was a UFO, large in size

It was so bright
It suddenly caught my sight
I saw an alien so far
Which made me think of a chocolate bar.

Monali Patel (13)
The Swaminarayan School

RABBITS

Nobody imagined
that the hopping of a rabbit
would alter the hunter
or the chewing up of a carrot
would bring its death.

Rabbits look out as
hunters hunt
in the green landscape
to search for a
rabbit hole.

Rabbits die day by day
which hunters have killed
every now and then.
So why do we care?
They're just old rabbits.

They don't come down
in the sky so bright
they don't come
flying down like
the rain in a cloud.

Reena Ved (12)
The Swaminarayan School

ENDANGERED SPECIES

Precious emerald forest, your beauty is beyond belief,
The canopy of green protected the treasures beneath,
Until the arrival of the twenty-first century highway man,
His muscular men arrived with force,
The roar of the saw, the sparks from deadly machinery
Made the forest animals flee in terror!

He tempted the traditional tribesman,
He offered sums of money beyond belief,
Promises or a rich man's life changed their values,
The consequences of their actions were forgotten.

Forest creatures are becoming extinct,
No longer the sound of chattering monkeys,
Just the grating of the saw,
No longer the glint of a jaguar's eye,
Just the reflection from burning headlamps.

Emerald forest, when will you return?

Jignesh Patel (12)
The Swaminarayan School

THE RAINBOW

Once I saw a rainbow, so colourful and bright,
I saw it in the morning, in the morning light.
It had strips of colour - yellow, red and green,
When you see it, you'll know what I mean.

It was a great big semicircle in size,
The sun was behind it - I saw it with my own eyes.
I gazed out of the window at it,
It looked as if it were lit.

The rainbow was such a beautiful sight,
I dreamt of it at night.
It was the highlight of the day,
I hurtled outside - there it lay.

Krishma Patel (10)
The Swaminarayan School

ME AND DAD

T hanusiya is a kind and generous girl
H elping people who are lonely
A nd likes English, history, DT, IT and reading
N ow she is studying in yar 7
U nbelievable thing is; she is taller than her mum and dad
S he does not like maths, geography, French or Gujarati
I t is very nice to be with her
Y ou can tell any secrets and she will keep them safe
A nd she is the kind of friend you would like

J eeventhira is Thanusiya's dad
E ven though he acts like God around me,
E asy to make him work for anything
V oted for Tony Blair to win the election
E lephant is his favourite animal
N ow he works in the Heathrow airport Royal Mail
T he favourite programme on TV is news
H ehas four sisters and two brothers
I n education his favourite subject is maths
R eal favourite sport is football
A nd loves going abroad for holidays.

Thanusiya Jeeventhira (11)
The Swaminarayan School

MANCHESTER UNITED

M agnificent
A lways spectacular to watch
N ever boring
C onsistent week in, week out
H ardly short of skill
E normous support around the world
S ir Alex, you are the best
T eddy Sheringham, why did you leave?
E lectrifying pace from Veron
R ed Devils rule

U nited are the best
N o contest in The Premiership
I ncreasingly getting more talented by the minute
T he best team in the world
E ver popular
D on't worry, we'll still perform when Sir Alex leaves.

Mahul Patel (11)
The Swaminarayan School

SUMMER

S ummer is scorching!
U nlike winter, you can wear anything.
M any kids play outside,
M aybe kids can get ice cream.
E veryone has fun,
R ound the clock, it is hot.

Prakash Halai (12)
The Swaminarayan School

Scared

I'm scared, I'm scared,
I'm scared of heights.
I'm scared, I'm scared,
I'm scared of death.
I'm scared that one day I'll end up like Macbeth.

I'm scared, I'm scared,
I'm scared that I'll fall, fall off a ladder
Or scared that I'll be bitten by an adder.

I'm scared, I'm scared,
I'm scared of a disease,
I'm scared, I'm scared, I'm scared I'll be on my knees.

I'm scared, I'm scared,
I'm scared of pain,
I'm scared, I'm scared, I'm scared I'll die in vain.

Mukesh Patel (14)
The Swaminarayan School

Rainbow

R ed rainbow, relaxing, resting in the raining, raining sky
A n ancient, amazing, acrobat eating an apple
I ndigo, Indian in an igloo introducing instruments
N ine nations nagging, nicking, knitting, naming and numbering each other
B ig, blue buzzing books, baking black boxes whilst barking and biting
O verall octopus, oblong, hates owls and loves October
W hilst wrestling, writing, wailing, winning, you wanted to be a wild wise whale.

Sanjay Patel (11)
The Swaminarayan School

The Weather Monster

(Dedicated to my unborn cousin)

The lightning is the weather monster, angry,
The thunder is him stomping,
The rain is him crying
And the wind is him sighing.

The fog is the steam from his bath,
The clouds are his pillow,
The hurricane is him sneezing
And the earthquake is him falling.

Finally it is sunny,
He is no longer naughty,
He is happy.

Amit Patel (14)
The Swaminarayan School

Twin Towers

T he twins together,
W ith pride they stand.
I nside are people working away,
N ever did they know the oncoming moment

T hat a plane was heading their way.
O n September 11th they crashed to the ground,
W ith people inside, all trapped underground.
E veryone wondering why it happened,
R ubble and bodies was what remained on that terrible day.
S hattered hearts is all that's left.

Paul Oumade-Singh (11)
The Swaminarayan School

RASHMI

(My mother, based on Mother's Day)

R avishing, red roses arriving home for you,
A n amazing angel awakening me.
S weet-smelling savouries bought for you,
H er heavenly hair hangs short.
M other's Day is a memorable, magical day just for you.
I ndoors and outdoors, incredible joy flows.

P oems and words cannot describe my love for you,
A n amazing, astonishing, Indian dinner.
T remendous, unbreakable, tight bond between you and me,
E veryone's enjoying eating your wonderful dinner.
L ove you lots for years to come.

Shiel Patel (11)
The Swaminarayan School

THE CREATURE

T he creature distracts us with its venomous claws
H e frightens away any human being
E xclusive, arrogant attitude it shows

C auses hazardous accidents each day
R apacious for food
E ar-splitting growls it has
A ddicted to humans and all their species
T hreatening, disobeying expressions it has
U tters thunderous growls
R espect the creature with fear
E ven though it will not harm you.

Ankur Joshi (13)
The Swaminarayan School

WATCH THAT CAR

Watch that car go over the bridge,
Watch that car get stuck in the ridge.
What that car whizz past in a flash,
Watch that car ending up in a crash.

Watch that car slow down at a turn,
Watch that car blow up and get burnt.
Watch that car go in for a check,
Watch that car coming out of the deck.

Watch that car go up a hill,
Watch that car turn into the mill.
Watch that car, it's rather wide,
Watch that car being hit on the side.

Himanshu Patel (13)
The Swaminarayan School

DEVIL'S NUMBER

The number was 666
Devil was born on the 6th
Comets fell and fires blazed
The sky fell, everyone gazed

The evil laugh shocked us all
The sun went out, no longer a bright ball
A red figure with red eyes
Which shot death that sprinted by

A heavenly light shone on us at an angle
Could it be that it was an angel
An angel it was, which saved us all
Defeating the devil with a love ball.

Rimal Patel (14)
The Swaminarayan School

VALENTINE . . .

It is a moon wrapped in red paper
It promises light
Like the accurate dressing of love

It will blind you with tears
Like any lover
It will make you a reflection of sadness

Its fierce and strong kiss will
Stay on your lips
As long as you live

Its valuable loops shrink into a ring
If you wish
Its scent will cling to your fingers
Then it will lose you forever.

Parin Sheth (13)
The Swaminarayan School

FIREWORK

F laming, fiery, fierce, flying through the sky
I nvolving, Indian colours, flying through the sky
R ushing, rage, light up the night sky
E volving, entertainment, adventure, brushing against the sky
W orking, washing, whizzing, comets flying through the sky
O range, octopus, in the air
R ushing firework, exploding in the air
K razy fireworks light up the sky.

Neil Kalawadia (11)
The Swaminarayan School

THE TASMANIAN DEVIL

T he Tasmanian Devil, strong and proud,
A long with the tiger, with pride, he
S trides towards glory.
M oving towards his prey,
A n animal prays that
N o one, especially the
I nvincible Taz, is
A nywhere near them.
N o one can stop him, or even

D are to try, for
E scape is impossible.
V icious and vile, he
I s, *not* a
L ikely person you should mess with.

Tarun Patel (11)
The Swaminarayan School

THE ZODIAC

T his is a book called Zodiac
H igh from the sky it comes
E ncouraging people to 'zodiac'

Z odiac is full of wonderful poems
O ut in the dark night the stars are glowing brighter than ever
D o you know why?
I think I know, because they're put on the book's front cover
A mazingly the star signs are formed on the book
C an you find them?

Rakhi Patel (11)
The Swaminarayan School

PLANET EARTH

The human being thinks he is so
Intelligent, which he is
But according to what he is doing to Earth,
He is being a curse to it.

The human being invented the car,
It saves us so much time,
But after so many decades,
It is destroying our lives
By polluting the air
And occupying so much space for roads.

If no cars were invented, then
There would be no need for so many roads
And if there were not so many roads
There wouldn't be any deforestation

Deforestation makes me feel sad
For the animals because we are
Taking their homes away
But alas, humans still continue to do this
Think or imagine what it would feel like
If we were in the place of the animals
And suddenly someone just took our house away
Well, we can only imagine
But the people in Gujarat have experienced it

I think that God's message to humans is:
If we take homes away from other living beings
Then he will take our homes away.

Dhaval Mistry (12)
The Swaminarayan School

Love Is

Love is all about you and me
Together
We will always be
Love is happiness
Love is sweet
When I'm with you, you make my heart beat
Love is happy
Love is sad
It turns the good times into bad
But love is not always sweet
It doesn't always wake your heartbeat
It puts you down
It makes you sad
Love is sweet
But also
Bad.

Bianca Gordon (11)
Winchmore Secondary School

Hello!

Animals, animals, animals,
I love you,
Cute and cuddly mammals,
Oink, baa, moo!

Music, music, music,
I find it so cool,
It makes me feel the opposite of sick,
It wraps like a ball!

Acting, acting, acting,
Is so my type,
Acting, acting, acting,
Acting, acting, acting.

Melissa Nagi (11)
Winchmore Secondary School

LIFE IS A TREE

Life is a tree,
Being young is beautiful,
Spring brings blossom,
Life has just begun.

Life is a tree,
The mind starts to think,
Green leaves and sun mean summer,
Tests and adventures approach.

Life is a tree,
Music means happiness,
But my tears fall like autumn leaves,
Decisions and results make my skin go pale.

Life is a tree,
Elder means independent,
The winter snow cools my mind.
I'll turn a new leaf to bring joy,
Just before I rot or get turned into a wooden toy . . .

Hiral Khetia (11)
Winchmore Secondary School

A Boy Is Dead

A boy is dead
Did he have to die?
His mummy and daddy
Think about him every day
And they ask each other
Did he have to die?
He was only 10
He never lived to see 11
He could have saved the world
He could have become the world's most wanted criminal
Did he have to die?
This boy went on his trip to have a good time
To go to a place he would remember forever
He was on the highest mountain in Britain
Enjoying himself and thinking this would be a great story
To tell Mummy and Daddy
But now he wouldn't be able to tell it to them
Did he have to die?

Zara Fenton (13)
Winchmore Secondary School

Art

Art is a way of telling people how you feel
Art is a way of expressing your feelings
Art is a way of making colours sing
Art

Art is like the bright sun
Art is like a shining star
Art is like an ice cream cake
Art

Art is good
Art is fun
Art is great
Art.

Tony Curto (12)
Winchmore Secondary School

BOOM

Boom Down goes the building
My heart sinks
He's off to Heaven

Boom Down goes the building
My heart sinks
She's off to Heaven

Boom Down goes the building
My heart sinks
They're off to Heaven

Boom Down goes the building
My heart sinks
Why am I off to Heaven?

Boom Down goes the building
My heart sinks
I'm off to Heaven

Boom Down goes the building
My heart sinks
I don't want to go to Heaven!

Boom Down goes the building
My heart sinks
When are you going to Heaven?

Paloma Thomas (12)
Winchmore Secondary School

Lonely Pencil Case

Lonely pencil case
I'm all on my own
Got no friends
I always groan

My back is killing me with all that stuff
Rubbers and sharpeners
I have to puff

Everyone always chucks me about
I just want to scream and shout
But I can't, I'm frightened and scared
But really I was actually feared

Compasses and sharp pencils dig into my back
Now I really feel like a sack
I'm really upset, I don't know what to do
So please come and give me some food.

Ciydem Cafer (11)
Winchmore Secondary School

Christmas

Bells are ringing,
there're carollers singing,
bright lights are shining,
dinners are roasting.

Children opening presents,
with delight in their eyes,
people with their families,
eating mince pies.

It's over now,
no more bright lights,
Christmas is over,
until the next year to come.

Heather Stephenson (11)
Winchmore Secondary School

Why War?

Many have died,
Many are suffering,
Many have cried
And many feel sorrow.

It may never be forgotten,
It may never be controlled,
It may never be stopped,
It may never end.

We are at war they say,
Sunday it started,
But why did this start they ask,
What does this mean?

Many feel hurt,
Many lives have been lost,
Many are in grief
And many want revenge.

Many feel sorrow,
It may never end,
What does this mean?
Many want revenge.

Demran Ali (13)
Winchmore Secondary School

The Colours Of The Rainbow

Red is the colour of love,
When you're in love you fly above.
Blue is the colour of the sky,
When all the clouds go passing by.
Yellow is the colour of the sun,
When you're hot you eat a bun.
White is the colour of a kite,
Only flown on a windy night.
Green is the colour of the trees,
As a sway from the gentle breeze.
Pink is the colour of a coat,
When you're cold, shaking in a boat.
Purple is the colour of a flower,
You wouldn't want to eat it because it's sour.
Orange is the colour of a balloon,
Or even a round cocoon.

Charmaine Smith (11)
Winchmore Secondary School

The Final Game

The tension mounts as the whistle blows,
90 minutes of truth and dare,
We're 2-1 down with a minute to go,
One more goal will take us there,
When Beckham's goal echoed in the air.

We shout, we cry, we sing and scream,
Our dreams rest upon this team of men,
Our World Cup final team,
We've had our ups, we've had our downs,
But Jules Rimet we will be crowned.

3 lions, we will be bound,
The Jules Rimet we will be crowned,
We will be crowned,
We will be crowned,
The Jules Rimet we will be crowned.

Ian Bremner (14)
Winchmore Secondary School

HARDYZ 2X

WWF is the best
With the Dudleyz
And Matt and Jeff

Jeff does a swinging
Swanton Bomb, he misses
But Matt carries on

The Dudleyz are
Ready for a 3D
Lita jumps in
With a powerbomb pin

Matt has got
Buh-Buh Ray
For a twist of fate
Jeff's got D-Von
At his fate

The Hardyz are ready
For a Swanton Bomb
The Dudleyz are demolished
The Hardyz have won.

Eltayeb Abdelrazig (11)
Winchmore Secondary School

FORMULA ONE CARS

The greatest driver of all time, Michael Schumacher
Takes to the track to sit in his two million dollar super car,
With his V10 engine burning,
He's ready to blast-off the hot and humid track.

All the cars are ready to start,
Waiting for the five red lights to disappear,
The scorching, deafening revs,
The fiery exhaust pipes
And the support of the wild fans
Keeps everyone eager to start.

Rocketing off the line,
With humungous amounts of wheel spin,
Booting it all the way to the apex,
Storming into the pit lane,
Getting fuelled up,
Attacking all the opposition
And he's off to his 53rd victory.

Pavlos Orphanou (11)
Winchmore Secondary School

LOOKING DOWN FROM A SATELLITE

High in the atmosphere,
My laser eye could see
Seas crashing,
Cloud like cotton candy.

Moon like burning lampshade,
Burning stars are balls of gases
In outer space,
I'm like a flying bird.

People are like tiny micro organisms,
Looking up with wishful dreams,
Ants you can't spot,
But I can see a community of just a colony.

Chanhdnee Hurchund (12)
Winchmore Secondary School

GIRLS

Girls, girls, they're so fine,
Can never get them out of my mind.
Girls, girls, they're so cool,
They never used to go to school.

Girls, girls, they're so loud,
Can never keep up with all the sound.
Girls, girls, they're so sweet,
They always make my heart beat.

Girls bring love,
Girls bring joy,
Girls make me happier than a little toy.

Girls will be my beginning,
Girls will be my end.
Girls are what I live for,
Right to the very end.

Loucas Christodoulou (12)
Winchmore Secondary School

CIGARETTE

I stood still, straight
Among the others
The thing let bright light flood in as a door opened
I sweated as it pinched me
Water covered my legs as a cave closed on me
And fire burned my head
So I turned red with rage
I must've exploded because black things fell to the ground
I kept on getting sucked
And then pushed away, I let out fumes, I was so angry
The pain
I started shrinking
I got so small
The black things got bigger
Until I was gone
Now people step on me
They don't care
I'm nothing.

Panitsa Christodoulou (11)
Winchmore Secondary School

GERMS

They make you move
They make you snooze
They make you cold
They make you bold

Germs have invaded your friend
Germs have invaded your body
Germs have invaded your home
Germs have invaded your world

They make you itch
They make you twitch
They make you cry
They make you die.

Raymond Poon (11)
Winchmore Secondary School

LIFE AS A FOOTBALL BOOT

I am stuffed in a smelly bag
I am gasping for fresh air
The beam of light
But realised people were getting changed
O, the sight was so disgusting
I am chucked on the hard concrete floor
It was an enormous pain
I was dragged back
I was in a spiritual anger
I couldn't breathe
The smelly foot was shoved inside of me
The laces were as tight as the longest tie
I was sweating in horror as I walked up the concrete floor
I was tense
I stepped in the humungous pitch
I could hear the other shoes sniggering
Boom the blow of the whistle deafened me
I was swashed by the football
I dashed past the other shoes
I gave a mighty great kick
Goal! I shot the ball in the net
Goal! Goal! Goal!
The match had finished
I was jumping in delight.

Miles Sylvester (11)
Winchmore Secondary School

An Alien's Journey

An alien's journey to Earth,
To explore surfaces like Astroturf
And to tell his fellow aliens about the big blue ball
And about earthlings, short and tall.

Its rocket whizzed into space,
Controlling it like an ace,
The rocket speeding under the stars
And passing big red Mars.

The alien put on his safety gear
And dodged comets without any fear,
Not a bead of sweat coming down its face,
Even though it was in outer space.

Asteroids and comets passed now and again,
The alien making notes with its pen,
The rocket went fast, even weighing a ton
And riding it seemed great fun.

The rocket landed on Earth,
The alien can finally examine Astroturf!

Dario Zahirovic (12)
Winchmore Secondary School

Journey To Mars

My journey to Mars
Is under the stars,
I was whizzing through the comets smoothly and calmly,
Having fun while eating my salami.

I landed down on the planet,
Without any problem but the comets,
I put on my gear
And went onto the planet without any fear.

I jumped onto Mars
And saw a Martian.
So I ran back into my rocket
And shot off like a socket!

Fozrul Azad (12)
Winchmore Secondary School

LIFE WITH WORLD WAR 3

Invasion; bombing; death,
all caused by one person's greed.
Can they not be satisfied?
Are not enough people killed?

Gunboats; tanks; planes,
all weapons from the Devil.
Innocence, love and hope die,
not only this but living lives.

Is this one person's greed worth
another's life? How selfish.
Somehow I don't think so!

Pain; anger; remorse,
mutual feelings across the world.
Imagine families tearing apart,
ripping, parting, tearing apart.

Life would be very different,
see the hateful side of people,
a precious view only seen through
the windows of unhappiness.
Can you imagine our world in war?

Kayleigh Cooper (13)
Winchmore Secondary School

THE CRASH

It happened on the 11.9.01
At 8.30
The plane crashed in the tower
Everything was gone

It was in rubble
Everyone was gone
I never knew, who or what was alive
There was no sign of life

Life in New York was gone for a long time
Everyone was scared
No one knew what to do
I was terrified

I hope they know what they have done
They have spoiled our lives
They don't have a heart
My life is gone forever!

I'm scared
Why us?
Why did this happen?
I'm shocked

I can't believe this happened
What if they do it again?
It was horrible
My life is gone forever

I never did anything to them
But why me?
Everyone I knew was gone
Everything I knew was gone
I hope they know what they have done
My life is gone forever

Everything I loved is gone
Everyone I loved is gone
I can't believe this happened
My life is gone!

Noor Habib-Ullah (12)
Winchmore Secondary School

Goodbye

There's a girl all alone
And the glitter is gone.
As she crawls through the rubble,
Her thoughts spell trouble.

There's a voice out of reach,
Drowned by the tyres' high-pitched screech,
She really wants to be helped,
As she screamed, shouted and yelped.

Ignoring the cuts and bruises,
Her energy she uses
To push away a large stone,
As she breaks her arm's bone.

It's not too complex,
Of what will happen next,
On her back; there she'll lie,
Wanting to say one last goodbye.

Everyone wants to get even,
For the loss on September eleven,
To take revenge for that girl who was all alone,
And now . . . she's gone.

Tina Christodoulou (13)
Winchmore Secondary School

The Forest

Morning comes,
The woods glisten in the dim morning light,
Tiny pearls glisten as they rest upon leaves and flowers,
Sparkling and shimmering,
The birds fly high,
I can hear their hungry cry.

As morning fades,
The pearls roll off the blades,
Onto the ground they fall,
Disappearing on contact,
The leaves are dancing in the gentle breeze,
Twirling and whirling,
Around and around,
The leaves dance with each other,
How gracefully they move.

The sun is high,
It smiles as it rests in the sky,
The leaves are green,
Curling in the heat,
Shadows are short,
My hands are clammy,
Oh, how I love this place.

The shadows are long,
I can hear the bird's spectacular song,
The breeze is colder, almost icy,
I don't want to go.

Up in this tree,
I can clearly see
The golden aurora,
Oh, how romantic it would be,
If I had someone special with me,
The glow is magical,
Almost unreal,
What a magic sight,
It almost made me forget about this great height.

I turn around,
Still listening to that familiar sound,
They are back,
It is them,
I fear this sight I shall never see again,
For this is the last magical night,
Now I see those little lights
And the glistening of their wings,
Goodbye my friends,
When this tree ends
Tomorrow, you will be no more.

Hayley Burgin (11)
Winchmore Secondary School

Clouds

Black and white clouds travelling day and night
Covering that bright light
Thundering through a dark night
Birds turn directions to see the great sight
Babies crying in fright
People dying from flying a kite
Thunder is a frightening light.

Christopher Ioannou (12)
Winchmore Secondary School

Life Of A Football

I was alone in a dark cupboard, dusty and cold,
There was a big match on tonight
And I was going to be in it.
Suddenly,
A flashing light shot me in the eyes
And then a shadow covered my head.
Two big hands crouched
Over me and picked me up.
I was in the hands of Michael Owen,
He dropped me on a big, wet, green muddy field,
I was getting kicked around,
I was put on a white spot,
I gigantic foot came out of nowhere and kicked me,
It felt like I had got stabbed with a knife.
At the end of the match I felt like
I was going to die,
I saw those mammoth hands again,
They grabbed me and pushed me into a cramped bag,
I couldn't even breathe
And there I was back in that dark, dusty, cold cupboard.

Luke Cook (11)
Winchmore Secondary School

News Terror

Lots of people were killed
They must be frightened
They must be scared
When the Twin Towers were clasping

Lots of people were screaming
Lots of people wanted to get out
But not all of them made it
That sure was a terrible sight

Children were crying
Ambulances were arriving
And the fire brigade
People were in horror

No one knew what to do
No one knew what to say
Everyone was terrified
Everyone was scared.

Sana Hamid (14)
Winchmore Secondary School

A Life Of A Pencil Case

I'm in a dark and gloomy school bag,
I'm always sitting there next to school letters, books and detention slips,
I am very lonely because there are no other pencil cases I can play
or talk with.

Suddenly the zip of the bag will open!
Some of the books will be taken out and some will stay.
Then more books will drop in!
Crash! Bang! Wallop! Ouch!
Then I will be shaken about as if the boy was running with the bag.

Soon the bag will open again and I will be slammed onto the desk,
I am in school. The bell rings to show it is time to go home.

The bag will be moving, the bag zip will open again.
I'm at home, sometimes I get a long rest.
The bag will not open until the next morning.
Sometimes me and the homework will be taken out.
Soon it will be night-time, I get to rest and sleep for 10 hours!
Finally it's night!
Goodnight!

Khayrul Islam (11)
Winchmore Secondary School

My Uncle

(Dedicated to Jason Lewis)

Why, oh why did you have to die?
Now all I do is sit and cry
You were so kind, so unique
No one compares, no matter how far we seek
Your smile, your jokes, your funny ways
I thought forever they were here to stay

Two and a half years have gone by
And I still ask that question, why?
So very polite, so well-mannered
Not a bad word unless West Ham got hammered
Yes West Ham, you were their number one fan
Now I'll support them for you the best way I can

You should never have been taken from us
Try to get over this, I know I must
But to know that smile I'll never see again
Is a constant reminder that my heart's in pain
Never even had time to say goodbye
That's why I keep asking, why?

Cherelle Baker (11)
Winchmore Secondary School

Chocolate

Chocolate is my favourite food
I always eat it when I'm in a good mood
Cadbury's is my favourite make
I especially like their chocolate Flake

I really like the creamy taste
I would never put it to a waste
I always stop in at the shop
Once I start to eat it, I can never stop

Wonka bars are what my friends buy
They say I should give them a try
Give up Cadbury's, no way
Maybe I'll try it another day

Chocolate is a special treat
Even though it's bad for my teeth
I will never give up chocolate any day
Not even when my teeth are rotting away.

Camilla Phillips (11)
Winchmore Secondary School

Acrostic Poem

J is for a jaguar, pouncing on its prey.
O is for an octopus, waving its eight long arms.
H is for a hamster, running on its wheel.
N is for a nanny goat, eating at your clothes.
N is for a newt, scurrying across the water.
Y is for yet more of these cool creatures to follow.

C is for cobra, spitting poison.
H is for horse, galloping across the horizon.
R is for rabbit, merrily hopping.
I is for iguana, striking out its long tongue.
S is for seal, balancing a ball on its nose.
T is for tiger, killing the prey.
O is for owl, sleeping all day long.
D is for dog, barking in the dark.
O is for ostrich, running across the golden sand.
U is for unicorn, galloping gracefully across the sunset.
L is for lamb, chewing the grass.
O is for otter, swimming in the dark grey water.
U is for this unique poem.

Johnny Christodoulou (11)
Winchmore Secondary School

Rock The Croc

Rock the croc has ears that bend,
And teeth that you can mend.

His back is full of green,
And surely he is mean.

His nose has two black holes,
And he can snap in half two poles.

His tail is full of scales,
Like a box of nails.

When he whimpers the wind blows,
And when he yawns the sea flows.

When he bites he's ready for a fight,
But when it's cold he's out of sight.

When he sleeps he snores aloud,
When he wakes he sees the clouds.

Shahel Khalique (12)
Winchmore Secondary School

A Man Of Wisdom

There is a man in a suit
He wants to impress everyone
His suit is traditional charcoal
This is all part of his brilliant performance

He wants to help us all
By telling us about the fool
This will guide us as to what we need to do
Let's work together to fight it too

This man sounds familiar
This man is of great importance
He needs to keep this country going
In order for it to keep flowing

He stands with such air
His name is Tony Blair
He is our Prime Minister
We must stand united.

George Ioannou (14)
Winchmore Secondary School

CHOCOLATE

I love chocolate,
You would be mad not to
It's so comforting and so sweet.

I love chocolate,
It gives me pimples
Every time I eat it.

I love chocolate,
I would never give it away,
It's full of love and it's mine.

I love chocolate
And it's all mine,
The delicious, scrumptious brown chocolate.

I love chocolate,
I'll never give it away,
So go away.

Melanie Kyprianou (11)
Winchmore Secondary School

TERRORISTS AT WAR WITH AMERICA!

T errorists bomb a place or two,
E verybody screams,
R ound the streets,
R ound the square.
O ften they use planes,
R am them into big, tall buildings,
I nto fields and trees,
S ome are lucky to survive,
T housands of people die,
S uddenly we're at war.

A merica strikes with bombs and missiles,
T errorists fight back, fast and furious.

W e have to put up with a war,
A nd we have to put our lives on the line,
R eally we do care.

W ill Bush attack?
I n violence or in civilness,
T ony Blair will get involved, try to
H elp, but that is just more problems.

A ll countries united,
M orocco, Greece and Japan,
E veryone is mourning,
R olf Harris, Britney and Lopez,
I think this is a national tragedy,
C oming from afar,
A ll the world is at attention, maybe Mercury and Mars.

Paul McRae (14)
Winchmore Secondary School

In The Dark, Damp Room, Nothing To Do

Sitting
In the dark, damp room
Nothing to do.

Listening to the clock
Striking twelve
From above my head.

It's getting darker every minute
Looking across the dark hall
Into the kitchen
Splash
As the tap started dripping
On the hard metal sink.

The tap is dripping by itself.
No one is coming to turn it off.

Thinking, just thinking, nothing to do,
No one is coming to turn
The cold sad tap off.

It's getting colder, the window
Is open, the curtain is
Blowing.

Sitting
In the dark, damp room
Nothing to do.

Cherice Clarke (12)
Winchmore Secondary School

KAYLEIGH SMYTH

K is for all the kindness in my heart
A is for all my amazing thoughts
Y is for all the youth in me
L is for all my love for my family
E is for all my good effort
I is for all my intelligence
G is for all my generosity
H is for all the happiness

S is for my super spacious mind
M is for all my good manners
Y is for all my young ability to learn
T is for all the tenderness in my heart
H is for all the happiness in my life.

Kayleigh Smyth (11)
Winchmore Secondary School

MY ACROSTIC POEM

Y eliz Mustafa is my name,
E very day is the same,
L aughing and giggling all day long.
I live in a
Z esty world.

M ust always get to school on time,
U sually watching programmes all the time.
S inging along to all different songs,
T alking to friends on the phone,
A lways arguing with my sister,
F riendly to all,
A s I say, my name is Yeliz!

Yeliz Mustafa (11)
Winchmore Secondary School

HAPPINESS IS . . .

Happiness is birds in a tree,
Happiness is between you and me.
We have something special,
So don't throw it away,
Because we need each other at the end of the day.

Happiness is a smile on your face,
Happiness is winning a race.
Happiness is a new baby brother,
Where did it come from? My mother and father.

Happiness is the birds and the bees,
Happiness is my beautiful knees.
Happiness is hearts and kisses,
Happiness is fishes and dishes.
Now think about this one more time
And tell me if you like this rhyme.

Eleni Hadjiminas (11)
Winchmore Secondary School

ERAY FEYZI

E ray Feyzi
R uns like crazy
A nd is lazy
Y ou're not like Eray Feyzi, crazy, lazy.

F eyzi is my second name
E ray is my game
Y ou're not in my frame
Z ebras are not to blame
I am on my aim.

Eray Feyzi (11)
Winchmore Secondary School

The Life Of A Book

I am a book, a sparkling book,
On a shelf, I am the newest.
Everyone stares at me, I feel so guilty,
It's like I've done something bad.

Then a hand grabs me and opens me,
I feel so refreshed, it feels so nice,
After a long time I fall asleep,
I wake up in a box, it's stuffy,
I can't breathe, I'm suffocating.

I feel a presence nearby, another book,
I stare, I look, I can't see a book,
I am all dirty, I am torn,
I am miserable, I am sad,
I am angry, I am lonely.

Bogdan Kireeve (11)
Winchmore Secondary School

Oops

D aryll is my name
A m I going for fame?
R oar the people will
Y ou can race my girl Gill
L ink her arm
L earn the rules

R un Gill, run
O ur people will cheer
S o Gill will put herself into 4th gear
E yes go down as Gill dies in fear!

Daryll Rose (12)
Winchmore Secondary School

My Father

The parlour needs papering but Father said it was a waste
to call a paper-hanger in and so he made some paste.
He brought a roll of paper, got a ladder and brush.

When Father papered the parlour he couldn't see there
for paste, dabbing it here, dabbing it there,
for paste the paper everywhere.

Mother was stuck to the ceiling, the children were stuck
to the floor, I've never known a family so stuck up before.

Soon Dad fell down the stairs and dropped his paper-hanger,
come on little Helen sitting there with a young man,
the paste stuck them together as we thought it would before life.

We had to fetch the person in to make the man and wife.

Sara Marie Spiteri (11)
Winchmore Secondary School

Burcu Yigit

B is for my bouncy ball
U is for my united stand
R is for my ravishing smile
C is for my clever mind
U is for my unlucky side

Y is for my youth
I is for my intelligent life
G is for my guitar
I is for my interesting music
T is for my TV.

Burcu Yigit (11)
Winchmore Secondary School

Why?

They left her cold and hungry,
In a bathtub she stayed,
Freezing cold she stayed,
Day and night with no shed of light.

Scars showed on her body,
That showed the pain she felt,
She must have cried out for help,
Why didn't anyone listen to a child so young and sad,
Why don't we open our eyes to all that is so bad.

Next time we should listen
To the cries of an innocent child
And give them all the love and support
That all children deserve.

Maria Yianni (13)
Winchmore Secondary School

Meanings Of Colours

Anger means red
and it's also like my bed.
Happy means yellow
and I like to eat marshmallow.
Jealousy means green,
when you're so, so mean.
Beauty is pink,
when the ships always sink.
Sad means blue
and it's the colour of your glue.

Eustacia Ramsawmy (11)
Winchmore Secondary School

PlayStation

Press the button and say good luck,
Watch yourself on the game,
Cos you can get lost if you don't,
Hear the music over and over,
Don't go that way,
Cos you can fall in me,
Damp your head on the lake near you,
Eat the grass and the fruits,
And make sure you staff yourself,
Cos you can die,
Run away from the evil,
Cos it can catch you,
Run, run, run, your life the evil spoke,
Then you get caught and you die,
Then you play again and again,
But you can't finish the game,
So play, play till you die.

Mahbubur Rahman (11)
Winchmore Secondary School

My Cat

My cat's name's Shadow because he's black
And he always comes to me when I'm listening to 2pac
He comes to me when I'm trying to sleep
And he creeps under the covers and scratches my feet
I like stroking my cat, but he's getting quite fat
That's because he eats a lot
My cat's very fluffy
And also very clumsy
But he's the best cat in the world.

Harry Michael (11)
Winchmore Secondary School

ACROSTIC POEM

V is for how vicious I am
A is for all anxiety
N is for all my neat work that I have written
I is for how intelligent me and my family are
S is for how shy I am
H is for how hard I work sometimes in class!
A is for how ambitious I am.

T is for how talented I am
A is for all the artistic work I have done
I is for all my independence
L is for all my loveable ways
O is for all the original stuff in my life
R is for how rubbish my art is.

Vanisha Tailor (11)
Winchmore Secondary School

TARA!

Tara, Tara, Tara your lips are so lovely and fine
When I look in your eyes and see what I see
I realise you're the only one for me
I love you so much
I need you so much
So let's love each other for life

Tara, Tara, Tara your personality is just fine
You make me laugh, you are so buff
We've got the strongest love.

Terry Webb (11)
Winchmore Secondary School

ACROSTIC POEM

T anyel is cool
A nd he likes to play pool
N ow he's rapping
Y eah, now he's tapping
E verybody come on now
L et's go to town

A nd play
L et's play
T anyel is tough
I nside he's rough
N o one uses stools
T anyel uses tools
A s they grow
S ome people are low.

Tanyel Altintas (11)
Winchmore Secondary School

MARCEL

Marcel is beautiful, like blue skies,
He has cute chocolate-brown eyes,
His fur is like a leopard's, all spotty,
He acts sometimes a little dotty.
He bites my hands twenty-four-seven,
When he cries his tears are from Heaven,
I couldn't leave him because he'd cry,
So would I, if he were to die.
He's a little crazy,
But that's not an excuse for being lazy!

James Martin (11)
Winchmore Secondary School

Chocolate

Chocolate, chocolate, chocolate,
I love chocolate,
Chocolate, chocolate, chocolate,
I can't live without chocolate.
Chocolate, chocolate, chocolate,
My life is chocolate.
Chocolate, chocolate, chocolate,
I can't go a day with chocolate.
Chocolate, chocolate, chocolate,
I dream about chocolate.
Chocolate, chocolate, chocolate,
Do you like chocolate?
Chocolate, chocolate, chocolate,
Chocolate is *everywhere!*

Eshreeka Pydiah (11)
Winchmore Secondary School

War, War

War, war has to end
War, war never again

War makes people feel for sorrow
And not want to live till tomorrow

War, war has to go
But never again, it had to blow

This devastating news
On this very shameful abuse

Needs to control the way
We socially live, from today.

Senel Ahmet (13)
Winchmore Secondary School

THE WAR

The night
is long and the stars are
out but the bombs are
shooting down from the sky

People worrying, crying,
running

The world seems to be filled
with badness but people
still don't want to die!

War is a bad thing, people die
don't you ever think why?
Why does it happen?

Why are people so unhappy?

Why are there bad things in life?

Why are people dying?
We're never gonna
know because people
can't be bothered to know

So we are always going to
stay with that thought
Why?

Ceylan Özsevim (13)
Winchmore Secondary School

LONELINESS

Loneliness is boring
You get terrified when you're by yourself
Sitting at home crying
Feeling scared when it's dark

When it's dark, when it's light, you feel haunted in your own house
Sometimes you go for a walk to clear your head
Instead of taking it out on other people
Loneliness is very unhappy
When you're feeling down about yourself
Sometimes you're so angry
You wish you had some company

Sometimes you just wish you had an interesting life
Instead of a boring and dull one
When you see other people happy
You get upset
You just want your life like that
When you're by yourself
You feel hurt and sad

When you have just lost your family
You feel bitter
So you take it out on yourself
When you're with a friend
You laugh and have fun

Sometimes when you're by yourself
You feel angry and mad
Your head's all over the place
When you watch TV
You see people
You say to yourself
One day my life will be like that.

Shewlee Kalam (11)
Winchmore Secondary School